WORSHIP, CHURCH AND SOCIETY

D.J. Brecknell

Whyke

10. viii . 93.

WORSHIP, CHURCH AND SOCIETY

An exposition of the work of
ARTHUR GABRIEL HEBERT
*to mark the Centenary of
the Society of the Sacred
Mission (Kelham), of which
he was a member*

by
CHRISTOPHER IRVINE

Foreword by
DONALD ALLCHIN
and
Epilogue by
PETER HINCHLIFF

The Canterbury Press
Norwich

© Christopher Irvine 1993

First published 1993 by The Canterbury Press Norwich
(a publishing imprint of Hymns Ancient & Modern Limited,
a registered charity)
St Mary's Works, St Mary's Plain,
Norwich, Norfolk, NR3 3BH

British Library Cataloguing in Publication Data

A catalogue record for this book is available
from the British Library

ISBN 1-85311-074-4

*Typeset by Datix International Limited
Bungay, Suffolk and
Printed and bound in Great Britain by
St Edmundsbury Press Limited
Bury St Edmunds, Suffolk*

AN APPRECIATION

'I want to express my gratitude for what you are saying to your readers about the important ecumenical contribution of Gabriel Hebert.

'I remember how, when we were gathered at the Anglo-Scandinavian Conference, we received the sad news that Father Hebert had departed from this life. Many of his friends, Scandinavian and English, were present, and we were all very moved. In our prayers we thanked God for what he had done for all our churches.'

– *Professor Lars Osterlin, University of Lund, Sweden*

CONTENTS

ACKNOWLEDGEMENTS

I am indebted to Canon Donald Allchin, who first suggested that something ought to be written on Gabriel Hebert, and who kindly agreed to write the Foreword to this book. I must also express my gratitude to Professor Peter Hinchliff, who kindly read the typescript and agreed to write the Epilogue. Helpful advice concerning the material which formed the basis of chapter two was given by Professor Lars Osterlin, of Lund University, Sweden. I also received much help from Dr Davis McCaughey, of Melbourne, Australia, who kindly placed three interesting files of correspondence and documentation at my disposal. It was a privilege meeting Dr McCaughey during my sabbatical leave in Australia, and I must thank the brothers of the Australian Province of the Society of the Sacred Mission for their hospitality. I was forcefully reminded by one brother that the life-blood of the Church is the hope of God's Kingdom, and the conviction that God is at work in his world; a vital SSM view, and the perfect remedy for ecclesiastical claustrophobia.

In England, I must thank Margaret Dewey, the SSM archivist at Willen Priory for her help as I began to research for this project. Canon Vincent Studwick has shown constant interest and support, and George Every, beloved of many generations of Kelham old students was a mine of information. Chapter five of this book is an expanded and reworked version of an article 'Reading the Bible as Scripture' which was published by the Sisters of the Love of God, in the *Fairacres Chronicle*, (Summer 1991). I take full responsibility for what I have written. The book was not intended as an academic study, and for this reason I have kept the notes to a minimum. Some of the figures I cite might appear larger than life, but I hope that I do not misrepresent them.

Last but not least, I must thank my colleagues at St Stephen's House for enabling me to take a sabbatical term in the summer of 1992, and Rosie, Ruth and Beth, for their good humour and tolerance in accepting a new, albeit invisible, member of our family. Gabriel Hebert was, of course, a member of the Society of the Sacred Mission, and it is to the brothers of that Society that I dedicate this book.

CHRISTOPHER IRVINE
St Stephen's House, Oxford

FOREWORD

In the middle years of this century, the religious communities of the Church of England produced three theologians whose work has had a remarkable influence on the life of the church in this country and beyond. There was Gregory Dix of Nashdom Abbey, whose *The Shape of the Liturgy* altered our vision of what the eucharist is. There was Lionel Thornton of Mirfield, whose *The Common Life in the Body of Christ* was one of the most substantial products of the school of biblical theology, a work which strengthened and deepened our understanding of the church. There was Gabriel Hebert of Kelham, the subject of this study by Christopher Irvine, not such a massive scholar as the other two, but one who encompassed many different fields.

I first met Gabriel Hebert when I was an undergraduate. There was more than forty years distance between us, but his gift for friendship was such that there seemed no distance at all. He was the most accessible, helpful and eccentric of friends. I couldn't help being impressed by the apparent lack of self-importance on the part of an internationally known writer whose books appeared in the catalogue of Fabers alongside those of T.S. Eliot. Still more impressive to me was the simplicity with which, towards the end of his life, he accepted his community's decision that he should go and teach in Australia.

It was after his return from Australia that I got to know him best. He was a many-sided person and could often be disconcerting. There was the curious childlike (was it childish?) streak in him. The last time I met him in London we went to have lunch with my parents in their flat in Earl's Court. Gabriel had just been given a large illustrated book of gospel stories for children. After lunch he insisted on my mother sitting on the sofa with him while he explained the pictures to her, as to a six-year-old. 'Look, there's Jesus sitting in the boat. I think that must be Peter, don't you? He *is* looking pleased.'

Then there was the last visit to Scandinavia, when I was with him for part of his journey. The respect and affection which his Scandinavian hosts felt for him was very clear. This was particularly the case in Sweden, in Uppsala and at Sigtuna, for instance, where he had many friends from the 1930s. But it was the same in Denmark, where Regin Prenter had arranged a memorable visit to Aarhus. At Sigtuna, the widow of Archbishop Brilioth, she was also Soderblom's daughter, came with her brother, a retired diplomat, to see him. There was a notable conversation about the Second Vatican Council, which had just begun, and the new involvement of the Catholic church in the ecumenical movement. 'My father always knew it would happen,' the old lady said, 'My father always knew it would happen.'

As Christopher Irvine points out, Gabriel was an uneven lecturer. I remember one occasion, for instance, when he seemed altogether to have failed to take the measure of his audience, and there was a subsequent sense of disappointment. But it was not always like that. I was with him at Worth Abbey, in the weeks immediately before the opening of Vatican II. The occasion is etched in my memory because it was the first time I had taken part in such an Anglican–Roman Catholic meeting *in England*. It seemed so strange to be engaged in such conversations with eggs and bacon for breakfast instead of coffee and croissants. Gabriel's paper dealt with the Old Testament roots of the elements of eucharist and anamnesis in Christian worship. God's people acknowledge in prayer their own sins and shortcomings, but that acknowledgement is swallowed up in their grateful recognition of God's grace, which abounds and redeems our human foolishness. And then he left his prepared text and with a mixture of emphasis and eloquence added a new paragraph. 'And when in God's time, the churches are truly reconciled and we can come together at one in the eucharist, will not God put a new prayer into our mouths, as we are able to look back over the centuries of our separation and see how through them God's greater purposes of good have been worked out?' It was a moment of utterance in which the various strands in his life's work, the study of liturgy, the investigation of scriptures, and the ecumenical movement all come together in one. It was a moment one could only feel in some way to be prophetic.

It is one of the virtues of this book that it shows the many-sided character of Gabriel Hebert's work and sets it against the background of his own time and place. It was a time and place very different from our own. The Roman Catholic Church, as opposed to occasional Roman Catholic theologians, stood massively apart from the movement towards Christian unity. Relations between Anglicans and Nonconformists (we were learning to call them Free Churchmen) were still coloured by memories of the polemics which had marked the previous century. The Student Christian Movement was still a major force in the Christian life of Great Britain, a training ground for the future leaders of all the mainstream Christian denominations. Britain itself was still the centre of a worldwide empire and few people had any inkling how soon that empire was to dissolve.

In such a situation it was very easy for Anglicans to be self-satisfied and insular. This was just what Gabriel Hebert was not. His early missionary experience in South Africa opened his eyes to what we now call the Third World. His pioneering exploration in Scandinavia brought him into contact with a whole world of Lutheran church life and theology of which most people in this country were wholly unaware. His lively appreciation of the liturgical movement as it was developing in continental Catholicism in the years between the wars, both in France and Germany, gave him a vision of Christian worship which was exciting and new, a vision which he managed to communicate to many of his fellow countrymen. As the title of his best-known book, *Liturgy and Society* suggests, it was a vision of worship not as a specialized and limited activity, but as a focal point for human society as a whole. Towards the end of his life in the 1950s he moved to Australia and in that remarkable episode had perhaps greater public influence than at any previous time in his career.

It was a life of very varied interests and it embodied a particular Anglican apprehension of Catholicity which was rooted in the life and worship of the community to which he belonged, the Society of the Sacred Mission, and in the vision of that extraordinary and prophetic man, H. H. Kelly, its founder. Christopher Irvine has put us all in his debt by this work of careful investigation and exposition which brings him to life for us again. At the end of this century Gabriel Hebert certainly still has things to say.

A. M. ALLCHIN

AUTHOR'S PREFACE

GABRIEL HEBERT is probably best remembered for his book *Liturgy and Society*, published by Faber in 1935. Inspired by a vision of the catholicity of the Church, Hebert became an ecumenical pioneer. But this book is neither biography, nor is it a historical study.

At a time when the ecumenical cause seems for many to be either running out of steam, or worse, radically off course, and when others are questioning whether the Eucharist ought to continue to be the central act of Sunday parish worship, it is imperative to consider again the insights and convictions of those who first moved the ecumenical movement, and who sought to establish the Parish Communion in the first half of this century.

Through a re-reading of Hebert's writings, Christopher Irvine identifies and critically evaluates a number of these convictions, including:

– the view that a genuine ecumenism asserts our unity in Christ, and yet in its desire for the fulness of Christ's truth, gives ample room for the plurality of Christian traditions;

– the belief that ecumenism should be based upon an adequate ecclesiology, which sees the historically given structures of the Church as a focus for unity;

– a view of the empirical Church as being constituted as the People of God when Christians gather for worship, and of how worship sustains a sense of Christian identity;

– an understanding of worship as the context in which the diversity of biblical literature finds a single voice as the story of God's people is rehearsed in the celebration of Word and Sacraments;

– an appreciation of the act of worship as the sphere in which Christians, united with Christ, are enabled to become co-workers with Christ in the making of a more humane society, modelled on the Body of Christ, in which individuals find themselves in relationships of mutual responsibility.

In discussing these vital convictions, this study seeks to draw the crucial connections between worship, church and society.

I
A CATHOLIC CHARACTER

BEFORE ATTEMPTING to expound the writings of Gabriel Hebert, and carry forward to our own times and circumstances the lineaments of his liturgical theology, we need first to set him in his own context, and to indicate the major influences upon his own life and thinking.

Family Background

If St Paul could claim to be a Hebrew born of Hebrews, Arthur Gabriel Hebert could claim to be an Anglican born of Anglicans. As the son of a Victorian clergyman he trod a predictable path; public school, and then on to Oxford, a year at Cuddesdon Theological College, and ordination.

Arthur Gabriel was the second son born to the Revd Septimus Hebert and Mrs Caroline Charlotte Hebert. Their first son, baptised Edward Noel, had died in infancy on 6 January 1885. At that time Septimus was the vicar of Silloth, in Cumberland, and in the summer of the following year, on 28 May, their second son was born. Arthur had two younger brothers, Godfrey, who was to become a distinguished surgeon and consultant at St Thomas's hospital in London, and Bernard, who was to be ordained later in life at the age of fifty-three. In 1889 the family moved south, and Septimus was inducted as vicar to the parish of Iver, a village in Buckinghamshire. At the age of seven Arthur was sent off to Cothill House, a preparatory school in Abingdon. As a young schoolboy, one of his most memorable experiences was meeting the great Mr Gladstone, whom his father admired greatly.

Although the immediate family was thoroughly Anglican, it had roots in French Protestant soil. When King Louis XIV revoked the edict of Nantes (which had granted religious liberty to the Huguenots in return for a solemn declaration of loyalty to the French monarchy), a number of Huguenots, including two brothers, Pierre and Robert

Hebert, fled to England. The two Hebert brothers eventually settled in Lincolnshire in 1686. Pierre, as the story went, returned to France, only to come to an unpropitious end by being executed by the villain of the Revolution, Robespierre. Arthur was intrigued by his family history, and as an adult claimed that his dislike of excessive Marian devotions was due to the Huguenot blood in his veins.

Both his grandfathers were clergymen. His maternal grandfather, the Revd William Haslam was a Cornish evangelical vicar, whose preaching and evangelical zeal made quite an impression on his rather sensitive grandson. Arthur's paternal grandfather, the Revd Charles Hebert had published a curious and rather dry book on eucharistic controversies. A flair for writing had obviously been inherited by his son, Septimus, who published five books. These books, with portentous titles such as *Whispers of Truth from the Stars*, and *Glimpses into Paradise*, reflected the Victorian preoccupation with death and speculative accounts of the after-life. His father also had a keen interest in astronomy, and when he died in 1931, Arthur inherited his rather magnificent telescope. There are many stories of how on a clear night, Gabriel would invite students at Kelham to his room to star-gaze, and how like an excited schoolboy he would point out to them the various stars and constellations.

At the age of twelve, Gabriel was sent to Harrow, where the regime was strict and formal. The boys were made to work hard academically, and there was a great deal of sport 'to round them off'. As was customary at the time, Arthur was prepared for confirmation at school, and was confirmed in November 1904. He enjoyed school and entered fully into its life. He gained a scholarship at New College, Oxford. There he studied classics, philosophy and theology, and left having gained a first-class degree in Theology. The Dean of New College at the time was Hastings Rashdall, an important figure in the history of English theology. The publication of his *Doctrine and Development* in 1898 is generally taken to mark the beginning of the English Modernist movement. The book itself is a collection of sermons, but significantly reveals the working of an eclectic theological mind. The Modernists were to be renowned for the way in which they wove together various strands of nineteenth century liberal thought. On the whole, they welcomed the so-called scientific methods of textual study, and combined the results of such study with an evolutionary model of history. The end result was the view of progressive revelation, the view that with the progression of time, and its inevitable increase in civilisation and sophistication, the divine nature can increasingly be shown and understood. Here then, was an essentially optimistic and Eurocentric theology, which was eventually to be rendered totally untenable with the release of sheer horror and human waste during the 1914–18 war. As T.S.Eliot declared in *Wasteland* in 1922, each epoch of human history could no longer be seen as an inevitable advance in human civilisation and progress; this realisation was the decisive deathblow for the Liberals' essentially optimistic world-view. Optimism was not the only legacy of nineteenth century Liberalism. There was also the tendency towards individualism, and within some Christian circles, the view that individual reason and conscience was the proper and sufficient arbiter in matters of belief and doctrine.

As an undergraduate Arthur was clearly influenced by these assumptions and currents of thought, and many years later he gave the following account of how, and why he came to distance himself from the Liberal outlook 'There are many of us in the Church who are seeking to make good our escape from the corrupting influence of Liberalism ... We are not reactionaries, taking refuge from the dangers of the future in a romantic return to the past. We do not shirk the issues raised by modern knowledge in the criticism of the Bible and in other regions of study, or by the political and social changes of the modern world, nor advocate a return to a closed theological system or to the political order of the past age. Nor do we fail to appreciate the virtues of the Liberal theologians, their desire to be honest and open-minded and to love the truth. It is rather that we believe that their Liberalism itself prevents them from doing justice to their principles; ... most of the opinions which I have myself criticised are opinions which I have myself held at one time or other, in my undergraduate days and since. The way out of Liberalism is not backwards but forwards'.[1]

Towards Ordination

Having graduated from Oxford in 1909, Arthur spent the best part of the following year working as part of the team at Oxford House in Bethnal Green in the east end of London. Bethnal Green had its share of poverty and social deprivation, and Oxford House was one of the so-called University Settlements which had been established in London's east end. The team's work had been inspired by the example of such Anglo-Catholic socialists as Fr Stuart Headlam. Oxford House provided space and facilities for the local residents, and was the base for its team of young graduate workers. The work of poverty relief was demanding and required a certain resilience in those who undertook it. There were various duties, including the distribution of shoes, food and clothing, and the running of a boys' club on the premises. During this time, Arthur was able to experience the ritualistic worship of the neighbouring Anglo-Catholic parishes.

In October 1910, Arthur went up to Cuddesdon Theological College, just seven miles from Oxford, where he spent a year in preparation for ordination. Little is known of his time there, but he kept in touch with his old college periodically throughout his life, and in his work *The Throne of David* (Faber, 1941), he alludes to a memorable college festival there in 1926, at which Bishop Charles Gore preached. In the spring before he died, he received a letter from Robert Runcie, then Principal of the college, asking if he would kindly consider conducting the old students' retreat which was planned for the summer.

At the end of his year at Cuddesdon, Arthur found himself moving north to a thoroughly working-class parish in what is now West Yorkshire. On Trinity Sunday, 1911, Arthur Gabriel Hebert was made deacon by Dr Eden, Bishop of Wakefield, and licenced to serve his title in the parish of St Peter and St Leonard, Horbury. The parish church was an uncluttered, light and spacious building, with a wide chancel and an apsidal sanctuary. The vicar, the Revd H.A.K-ennedy had been influenced by the Oxford Movement, and the Eucharist was given a prominent and central place in the worshipping life of the parish. There was a daily celebration of the Eucharist, (the vicar preferred to use the term Eucharist, rather than mass), and on Sundays there was the customary early celebration at 8.00 am, Sung Mattins at 9.45 am, followed by a Sung Eucharist at 10.30 am. Arthur considered Kennedy to be a good vicar and was grateful for the training he received from him in pastoral work. Like most young curates of his day, Arthur was obliged to write out a full script for his sermons, and these had to be shown to the vicar for comment and criticism before he preached them. The daily routine at Horbury followed the general pattern, with the greater part of the morning allocated to study, and parish visiting in the afternoons. After Evening Prayer there was usually some event or meeting which had to be attended. Responsibility for the church's work with children was deputed to Arthur. He had oversight of the Sunday School, and also taught two scripture lesson each week in the local elementary school, and on the announcement of his departure, the vicar wrote this tribute : '. . . he will have left in the church very definite marks of his work, particularly in the reorganisation of the Sunday Schools'.[2]

Links with the Society of the Sacred Mission

Arthur's first contact with the Society of the Sacred Mission, the SSM, was meeting Fr David Jenks, on one of his frequent visits to Oxford. Fr Jenks had succeeded Fr Herbert Kelly, the founder of the SSM, as Director in 1910. Having established the Society, and its primary work of theological education at Kelham, Kelly had announced, in a characteristically dramatic way, that it was time for him to bow out from centre stage. So, the chains of office fell to Fr Jenks, who made strenuous efforts to make the SSM better known and understood in the wider Church.

Arthur's first real introduction to Fr Kelly was through the articles he published in the SSM Quarterly, which he received when he was a curate in Horbury. Recalling those early days in a review of the 1959 SCM edition of Kelly's *The Gospel of God*, he tells how those articles in the SSM Quarterly, '. . . came as a living word, which stung me and annoyed me and provoked me by the way they presented the challenge of the living God, and the difference between loving God and loving myself and my own ideas and ideals; but I had to admit that he was right, and after a while I found myself at Kelham'.[3] Arthur in fact visited Kelham during his second year at Horbury, and Fr Kelly was obviously impressed by this intelligent young priest, and he was soon to become his protégé.

Herbert Hamilton Kelly, 1860–1950, was an unconventional figure with an independent mind. A series of failures had opened up his vocation, which was to mobilise for the Church's work the wasted talents and energy of the working classes, who because of lack of means and educational opportunity were generally overlooked by the Church of England. On 15 December 1890, having spent some weeks living with the brethren of the Society of Saint John the Evangelist, (the SSJE), at Cowley, in Oxford, Fr Kelly moved to 97 Vassall Road, in the parish of St John the Divine in Kennington, south London. There he began his life's work. The initial scheme, first suggested by Canon Scott Holland of St Paul's Cathedral, London, was to prepare young men to join the recently consecrated Bishop Corfe in the mission field in Korea. The work began with three students, and a strict regime of study, common prayer, and manual work. After an uncertain and faltering start, the college as conceived

in Kelly's mind began to grow: On Michaelmas Day 1893, Herbert
Kelly and Fr Herbert Woodward, an experienced missionary priest
who had been working in Zanzibar, in Central Africa, made their
profession as the first members of the Society of the Sacred Mission.
By 1897 the Society and its college had outgrown Vassal Road, and
moved to larger premises in Mildenhall in Suffolk. In 1903 the move
was made to Gilbert Scot's Kelham Hall, in Nottinghamshire. The
idea of the college to provide an opportunity for young men prevented
by their social and economic background from even considering a
vocation to the Church's ministry, was really Kelly's genius. He
refused to give a definite promise of ordination, but offered his
students a thorough theological grounding. The curriculum, from the
beginning, was broadly based, reflecting Kelly's wide interest in
human endeavour, and ranged from philosophy and psychology,
through to Christian doctrine. He wanted his students to think and
to think critically. In the *Principles*, which he first drafted in 1894,
and which encapsulates the ethos and outlook of the SSM, he had
said 'However many things it may be useful to know, the first object
of study is to discipline the mind to hold nothing either rashly or
vainly . . . Meditate much, for it is better to understand one thought,
than to repeat many words'. (*Principles*, VII). Alongside the demand
that students should think carefully and clearly, was set the challenge
of sacrifice, the requirement that they should seek to discern the
sovereign purposes of God and submit themselves in joyful obedience.

Professor Henry Chadwick has recently claimed that one of the
causes of the present 'crisis in the Church', is that she has lost a sense
of her own history. In his diagnosis, the Church is suffering from
institutional amnesia, and the situation is worsened by the fact that
church history has become the Cinderella in the world of theological
education. Such an accusation could never have been made against
the educational work of the SSM. From the very beginning at Vassall
Road, church history had been the constant component running
through the whole theological course. Kelly had passionately believed
that history was the stage on which the interaction between human
nature and the divine will was acted out. The object of the study of
history, in his scheme of things, was to give the student the ability to
read the present times, and to inculcate that historical perspective
which would prevent him from adopting an attitude of doctrinal fundamentalism.

As an undergraduate at Queen's College, Oxford, Kelly had come

across the writings of F.D.Maurice, (1805–1872), and this was undoubtedly one of the most significant discoveries of his life. He
found him to be an obscure writer, but felt an instinctive sympathy
with Maurice's suspicion of all systems of thought, both philosophical
and theological. Maurice himself had been a conspicuous figure in
the nineteenth century world of religious debate and theological
controversy. At one time or another, he had succeeded in raising the
ire of Evangelicals, Tractarians, and Liberals, and was removed from
a professorial chair at King's College, London, on the allegation that
he did not believe in hell. Maurice saw himself as someone who dug
deeply into the foundations of Christian life and belief, and his
genius lay in his ability to combine disparate insights into new and
fruitful combinations. For Kelly, the real value of Maurice's writing
was that it acted as an effective springboard for his own thinking.
On one occasion he said 'When I have read two pages of Maurice, I
have forgotten what he said. I am thinking so furiously for myself'.
From Maurice he learnt the important distinction between notion
and reality, the need to ask searching questions, to return to basic
principles, and finally a vision of the catholicity of the Church, its
inclusive universality. F.D.Maurice was undoubtedly the single most
important influence upon Fr Kelly's conception of theological education. Theology, he once said, is a view of the whole life, and in a
letter to the *Manchester Guardian*, he urged that theology needed to
be understood 'in a new and deeper sense, as a thing to be thought
rather than learnt, with a view to its being understood rather than to
its being merely correct'. Here indeed was a searching and creative
vision of theological formation, a vision which had to be translated
into practice.

Having resigned as Director of the SSM in 1910, Kelly was looking
for another opportunity to pursue his vision of theological education,
and an opportunity presented itself in the form of an invitation to
join the staff of the projected Central Theological College at Ike-
bukuro, near Tokyo, which was being sponsored jointly by the
SPCK, the CMS and the American Episcopal Church. Kelly received
the invitation early in 1912, when he was nearly sixty. They were
looking for three theological teachers, and Canon Scott Holland and
Neville Talbot had suggested that Fr Kelly should lead the team.
Kelly knew that if such a venture was to succeed, he needed to
recruit people he knew he could trust, and who would share his aims
in theological education. On 4 July 1912, Kelly wrote a rather
quixotic letter to Arthur Hebert at Horbury: 'Do you want to chuck

your life away for the sake of what is . . . the biggest option of the market?' The option was to build up the Central Theological College to be the nucleus of the Anglican Church in Japan, a church which from the beginning Kelly believed ought to be a Japanese church, and not the Church of England transplanted on to Japanese soil. For this reason, he wanted to recruit staff who he thought might have the ability to learn the Japanese language, but their primary task in the field was 'to make these children think'.

The invitation to join Fr Kelly in Japan had been unsought, and was not a little unsettling, but somehow the challenge was irresistible. Eventually a decision was made, but in seeking medical advice Arthur was advised not to go immediately, but to wait three or four years, as he was prone to be a little over-anxious, and the doctor who advised him did not want to risk a nervous collapse. The following year, 1913, Arthur was issued with a clean bill of health. Kelly set off for Japan; however, it was uncertain exactly when Arthur might join him. In the interim, it was decided that Arthur should go to Kelham and gain some experience of the Kelham method of theological education. He clearly did expect to join Fr Kelly, but realised the wisdom of serving a kind of apprenticeship at Kelham, before 'attempting to teach men of a different language and a different family of the human race on the other side of the world'.[4]

Arthur Hebert arrived at the House of the Sacred Mission, Kelham, in December 1913, and in the new year began his work as a theological tutor. With the outbreak of war, the possibility of joining Fr Kelly receded into the background, and life at home became increasingly uncertain. He became a novice of the Society on 8 July 1915, but the House was soon commandeered by the army, and so the brethren and the few remaining students who had been declared unfit for military action, went to live at the College of the Resurrection, Mirfield. During this period, Arthur would spend weekends helping in his old parish in Horbury, and stories concerning his inability to organise the simple practicalities of everyday life began to circulate. One of these stories was that he was so absent-minded about pyjamas and shaving gear that the only remedy was to have two sets and to keep one set at Mirfield, and the other at Horbury.

The SSM brethren returned to Kelham Hall in March 1919, and found it in a rather chaotic state. A number of the SSM brethren, novices, and students had been lost in the war, and consequently the college faced another staffing crisis. Kelly returned from Japan, concluding what was reputably the happiest and most effective episode in his whole career. Despite the enormous language barrier, he was understood by his students, and during this period managed to write the bulk of his book *Catholicity*. So, Kelly returned, and now literally as the 'Old Man', had to take on the full responsibility for the teaching of the four year church history course. Staffing problems at Kelham were exacerbated by the fact that the Society had to maintain its commitments and work overseas.

South Africa

In November 1920, Arthur, together with a priest and three other novices, set sail for South Africa. He had not been elected for Profession, and had failed to prove himself as an effective tutor in the college. In South Africa he was to be a missionary priest.

The Society's involvement in South Africa began soon after the Boer War, when they were invited to take over the running of an already established missionary settlement at Modderpoort, in the Orange Free State. Modderpoort, set in expansive country, was in the diocese of Blomfentein, and was regarded as being an Anglo-Catholic stronghold. The Tractarian influence was deep, but fortunately lacked the ritualistic fussiness and mannered style of its English counterpart. At the instigation of Bishop Twells, a missionary brotherhood, the Society of Saint Augustine, was recruited in England and arrived in Modderpoort in 1867. A farm had been bought by the bishop, but the community of seven brothers made a temporary home in a large cave, which later became something of an Anglican shrine. Eventually a chapel, and a stone-built house were erected, becoming the base from which the brothers operated, and providing facilities for rest and recuperation for the geographically isolated parish clergy. The community had to face many problems in its early days, but their biggest problem was that of recruitment. Without a home base in England, the Society of Saint Augustine was unable to ensure the necessary recruits to sustain its work. By 1908, the community was reduced to two priests and one lay-brother, and it was evident that the continuation of their work required them to be part of a larger organisation.

A Missionary Priest

Arthur arrived in South Africa on 20 November 1920, and the SSM contingent spent a couple of days with the Cowley Fathers in their

priory in Cape Town before making the arduous journey to Modderpoort. Modderpoort itself is set in the most visually stunning country-
side. In 1920, the priory was made up of a complex of buildings.
There was the priory itself, a church, and a number of cottages
housing the student catechists and their families. From the priory, a
vista opened up across the veldt to the distant Maluti mountains.
The newly arrived novices were given some time to acclimatise
themselves to their new surroundings; then for Arthur began the task
of learning the Sesuto language. This was no easy undertaking, but
he showed a certain linguistic flair, and by Christmas was able to say
mass in Sesuto.

The range of work covered by the SSM brethren in South Africa,
in the 1920s, and the extent to which the diocese of Bloemfontein
was dependent upon them, is well described in the following extract
from Bishop Walter Carey's autobiography:

> 'Bloemfontein diocese is as large as England and Wales,
> with one big town – Bloemfontein, with 25,000 whites and
> about 600 coloured. There are two or three middle-sized
> towns like Kroonstad, but the rest are "dorps", large
> villages, with a store, a church, a post office, and a
> magistrate, with 200–400 inhabitants. These lie about thirty
> miles apart, i.e. a day's trek in an ox-wagon. That is
> how they originated; resting places for trekkers. ... There
> were fifty clergy, about forty white and ten native, and
> the diocese was divided up between them. At Modderpoort
> there was a strong branch of Kelham – the Society of the
> Sacred Mission – and they superintended native work over
> a huge area; they also ran a school and trained ordination
> candidates. The usual plan was to station a priest at x
> and he lived there, but served – by car or horseback three
> other centres, A, B, and C. So he ruled over a
> quadrilateral of four little centres and gave them each a
> weekend every month'.[5]

The work was exacting, and there was plenty of scope for future
development, but the SSM was having to face and work through a
number of internal and domestic problems. A new Director had been
elected in the summer of 1920, and the election had been contested.
The brethren in England and at Kelham had voted unanimously for
the nomination of Fr Gerald Murphy, and the South African Province
had backed Fr George Carlton. In an attempt to force the issue, Fr
Murphy had made it known that he would leave the Society if Fr

Carlton was elected Director. In the event, the Great Chapter very wisely appointed Fr Joseph White, a mature man and experienced missionary, who had worked with the University Mission to Central Africa in Zanzibar. This move released a considerable amount of acrimony, and a number of issues which had been forced by the Anglo-Catholic tendency were unresolved. The crisis was not a straightforward crisis of leadership within the SSM, but was personalised and focused on Fr Carlton, the favoured man among those with a distinct Anglo-Catholic affiliation and outlook.

The underlying issues had arisen earlier in a contentious debate in 1918, which had revolved around the question of the reservation of the Blessed Sacrament, and more generally, the question of the nature of the religious life as it was lived in the SSM. On the subject of reservation, Fr Kelly was anxious for the society to be seen to follow the mind of the Church of England, and penned a memorandum to this effect, while he was in Japan. In setting out his own position, Kelly had said that although he had no objection to the practice, and fully appreciated its pastoral usefulness, he advised that the Sacrament should only be reserved in an SSM priory with the Director's knowledge and the consent of the diocesan bishop. Carlton was more militant on this issue, and argued that Anglo-Catholic convictions on the matter should dictate their policy.

Carlton was singularly responsible for raising the question of the nature of the religious life as it was lived in the SSM. On 15 December 1918 he issued a fourteen-page discussion paper, which posed the dilemma as to whether the SSM was a religious society, or an organisation for specific work. Kelly, who shunned all partisan spirit, was swift to reply with an open letter, entitled 'To my Brethren'. In this letter, Kelly reminded his brethren that the SSM was founded to serve the Church, and warned them in the strongest possible terms that partisanship was the danger to be fled from. Fr Carlton was more temperamentally suited to the style of religious life which had been adopted by Fr Benson and the SSJE, at Cowley, and towards the end of his controversy with the SSM Director at Kelham, he confided in a Cowley Father, and admitted that the SSJE had been his first love.

Fr Kelly had conceived the SSM as a means of organising the devotion of ordinary men, and as a religious society, the models to be looked to were the Oratorians and the Jesuits, and not the strictly monastic communities. The emphasis in other words, was to be placed upon the work of the society, and not its style of life. The differences between a religious society, such as the SSM, and a more monastic religious community, are probably best seen by comparing rites of Profession. From the beginning, the SSJE Profession had involved the traditional threefold monastic vows of chastity, poverty and obedience. The SSM Profession, on the other hand, consisted in the declaration of the new brother's intention to dedicate his life to 'the Divine Service', in obedience to, and within the society. In addition, provision was made for brothers to make a Life Promise. This was usually made after ten years of Profession, and those brothers who had made their Life Promise, were especially entrusted with the guardianship and preservation of the Society. Carlton felt that the SSM Profession was inadequate and undervalued the character of the religious life, but it seems that he never really caught the SSM spirit. Carlton was an intelligent, highly capable man, and returned to South Africa after the Great Chapter with undiminished energy and commitment to the work of the SSM there. The corporate life of the priory was tightly regulated under his leadership, but qualms and uncertainties remained. In January 1921 one brother left the Society in South Africa to become a Roman Catholic, and another followed soon after, and although these departures and the inconclusive debate about the very nature of the Society was unsettling, Arthur Hebert was not deflected in his desire to become a member of the SSM. After his first Easter in South Africa, the brethren met in chapter, and it was agreed that Arthur should begin his preparation for Profession. On 11 April 1921, he wrote a candid letter to his father, a letter which shows an impressive measure of realism and fortitude in his struggle with his sense of vocation:

> 'Our Society at home and abroad is by no means out of all its troubles yet. But it seems quite clearly right for me to go on: I am quite sure that the Society and its work is of God, and it would be faithless to draw back. As a matter of fact, I would far rather have the Society as it is now, amid all its troubles, than it was in the time before the war when it seemed so strong. In those days it was horribly cock-sure, and had very little idea of its real weakness, and of its need of God'.[6]

Arthur Gabriel Hebert was Professed on Michaelmas Day, 29 September 1921, and from then on was to be known as Fr Gabriel. His Profession retreat had been a happy experience, and after his Profession, Gabriel felt that he really was beginning a new life. As a professed brother, his life was full, demanding and purposeful. At Modderpoort, he was responsible for teaching a course on the gospels, and drafted a series of services to celebrate the rites of Christian initiation for adults. In the new year, he moved from Modderpoort to Kroonstad, and his work as a mission priest began in earnest. In 1923, he shared the pastoral work in and around Modderpoort, and was given special responsibility for the mission stations at Bethlehem and Frankfort, where the Eucharist had to be celebrated, confessions heard and advice given, as well as the solemnisation of marriages, Baptisms, (which often happened after the Sunday mass), and other pastoral offices. Once a quarter, Gabriel also had to make a fifty-mile trek on horseback to an old mission station at Hanbury. By anyone's reckoning this was a punishing work schedule, but Gabriel was a committed mission priest and gave himself unreservedly to the demands made upon him. Within the relentless round of duties and demands, he somehow found time to initiate new projects.

At Frankfort, for instance, Gabriel embarked on a project to build a more permanent church, and actually designed the building himself. The drawings were little more than sketches, but Gabriel was to supervise the builders himself. The foundation stone was laid with due ceremony on 20 May 1924, but from then on the work progressed very slowly. At certain stages in the construction, Gabriel had to work with the builders. The lintel over the main door was his design and his own work. Gabriel's father, Septimus, had raised money at home to meet the greater part of the cost of the building, and he had also managed to procure an unused church bell, and arranged for this to be shipped out to South Africa for the church at Frankfort.

Thus Gabriel had to fill a number of quite different roles. He was a teacher, a mission priest, a translator, and church builder, and inevitably conflicting demands were made upon his time, energy, and attention. So it is no surprise to find him, during a moment of introspection, on his thirty-eighth birthday, writing in a letter to his father:

> 'I am at present a compound of about five different personalities, in which I live alternatively, and am wholly absorbed in that one which I am in at that time. One of them is absorbed in the new Sesotho Prayer Book; another is keenly interested in buildings and thinks of nothing else except the bills; another is the mission priest of Bethlehem, another does college tutoring, but he is really interested in

the activities of the other personalities. Then I suppose, there's ME somewhere'.

It would be an exaggeration to say that this letter was indicative of an identity crisis, but clearly Gabriel did feel that he was torn in different directions, and this sense of personal unease would undoubtedly have been exacerbated by being caught in the internal controversies of the SSM. Unfortunately, Gabriel became a pawn in the various political manoeuvrings between Fr Carlton and the Director, in England, Fr Joseph White. On 7 March 1922, the Director wrote to Carlton indicating that Gabriel might have to return to Kelham. Carlton was horrified at the possibility, and in his reply, claimed that such a move would be seriously detrimental to the work of the Society in South Africa. Six weeks later, Carlton received a telegram from Fr White, informing him that Gabriel was to return to Kelham. Carlton responded immediately with a telegram, followed by a long letter in which he argued that if Gabriel was recalled, then their work in the northern part of the Free State would have to be abandoned. Carlton then ignored all further directives from Fr White, and handed the whole matter over to Bishop Walter Carey. After some correspondence between the diocesan bishop and the Director, it was eventually decided that Carlton himself ought to return to England, and that Fr White would sail to South Africa and take over the reins as Provincial there. Carlton sailed from Cape Town on 20 February 1923, and returned to England. In the following August he left the Society of the Sacred Mission.

At the time, Gabriel was unaware of what was at issue in the correspondence between Carlton and Fr White. He never baulked under Carlton's regime, but evidently felt some relief at his departure.

The strains of the work took their toll on Gabriel's health. His father visited him in November 1922, and was seriously concerned. Gabriel was physically exhausted, and had suffered a bad bout of 'flu, and in a letter to his wife, Septimus expressed his fear that 'a breakdown is bound to come'. On medical advice, Gabriel was ordered to take a holiday, and went off to spend a few weeks with the Johnstons, some friends of the Society who lived on the coast. Twelve months later, after Carlton's departure, Gabriel admitted in a letter to his parents that his illness the previous year had been caused 'not so much from overwork, as from not being inwardly happy'. In this same letter, he assured them that he was much happier in himself since Fr White had joined them at Modderpoort. Fr White was less preoccupied with the outward form of the religious life and with the scrupulous observance of rules, and more concerned to respond to the opportunities and difficulties of living and working in community. As Gabriel put it 'Fr White makes you get down to the realities of the Christian life'. Towards the end of that year, Septimus Hebert made his second visit to South Africa, and much to his son's delight, was able to be present at the Dedication of the Church of the Resurrection, at Frankfort, on 14 December 1924.

The following year, Gabriel was sent home to England on furlough, but he was never to return. Nevertheless, he always maintained a real interest in the work of his brethren in South Africa, and the needs of that country were always in his heart and prayer. In his first book, examining the question of Christian unity, he described South Africa as a country 'torn by deeper and more complex racial divisions than any other country in the world',[7] and went on to say that when blacks and whites in that country knelt together to receive Communion, there was a demonstration of Christian unity, and a prophetic sign of judgement on a divided and unjust society.

'Down Under'

The cultivation of eccentric behaviour is a well known and understandable strategy for coping with life in a large institution, and it seems as though Gabriel was particularly susceptible to this path of public behaviour. Human personality is a complex matter, and it is not uncommon to find contradictory elements combined in a single character. With Gabriel there was a strange combination of a highly developed intellectual capacity and a certain emotional immaturity, which showed itself as a naïvety in human relationships. He had a natural fascination for technical detail, whether it was the tonnage of a ship which had taken him across the North Sea to Scandinavia, or a toy train which he had spotted in a shop window, and he would talk of such things with a child-like enthusiasm and a child-like insistence that he should be the centre of attention. In this respect he was an adept and amusing teller of stories, but the laughter he raised from his audience, either sitting around a table in the refectory, or in the Common Room, was caused as much by his excited high-pitched voice as by whatever it was that he was recounting. More seriously, there were aspects of his behaviour which were less endearing, and which for many were deeply irritating. In chapel, for instance, there was his inability to sing in tune, and to keep in pace with others in the recitation of the psalmody. Undoubtedly too, as his reputation and esteem grew beyond the confines of the college at Kelham, so his attitude to his brethren changed. Gregory Wilkins once said that there was a marked change in Gabriel in the late 1940s when he realised that people outside the Society regarded him as being an 'authority'; but against this judgement, perhaps one should recognise that there were probably petty jealousies of both a professional and emotional kind, and ones which undoubtedly strained relationships between the brethren. Certainly one of Gabriel's most difficult relationships in this period was with Stephen Bedale's successor as Warden of the college, Theodore Smith. Although Theodore was an efficient administrator, he was no intellectual, and sometimes felt inadequate to the task of leading the college, and it is probably true to say that there was little real communication between the two men.

By 1950, it is fair to say that on the whole Gabriel, though held in great affection by the student body, was largely marginalised by the younger generation of tutors at Kelham. They were especially infuriated by what they considered to be his attention-seeking behaviour, not least the affected way in which he would walk around the House sucking the end of his blue scapular. So, in certain quarters there was a sense of relief when the newly elected Director, Paul Hume, announced in the autumn of 1952 that Gabriel was to be sent to join the brethren at St Michael's House, the recently established 'Australian Kelham', at Crafers in South Australia. Gabriel was very reluctant to go, and given his age, (he was now in his midsixties), his wide circle of friends and contacts outside the college, his reluctance was understandable, and he repeatedly told people at Kelham that they would miss him when he had gone. After the traditional missionary benediction in the Great Chapel, there was an immense and tearful goodbye in the car-park just before he was whisked off to Newark railway station for the first leg of his long journey to the Antipodes. Rather absurdly he returned to Kelham some twelve hours later, because of a seaman's strike at Southampton docks. In January, however, a passage was booked, and quite fortuitously, Gabriel sailed to Australia on the same ship as Dr Davis McCaughey and his young family. Davis had been a frequent visitor to Kelham in his capacity as an SCM secretary, and was well acquainted with Gabriel, whom he held in esteem. The coincidence of these two men sailing on the same ship was to be of considerable significance for Gabriel's time in Australia. During the voyage the two men struck up quite a friendship, and discovered that there was a considerable area of common interest between them. In conversation with Davis Gabriel sadly mused that while he was going out to Australia to die, Davis was going out to begin his life's work; but as the days passed, even Gabriel became a little infected by the excitement engendered by a long journey. As it happened, they were at sea for the Week of Prayer for Christian Unity, 18–25 January, and rather typically Gabriel managed to gather a group of Christians from various traditions to pray together each evening that week in his cabin.

Gabriel's friendship with the McCaughey family provided a basis for personal support, and once Davis had settled into his new job as professor of New Testament at Ormond College, Melbourne, an entrée into another circle of theological discussion. Throughout his time in Australia, Gabriel became a regular visitor at the Mc-Caugheys' house in Melbourne, and it was actually at a discussion around the McCaugheys' dining room table that the first plans were laid to inaugurate the Week of Prayer for Christian Unity in Australia. It will be seen, as the story unfolds in subsequent chapters, how natural and appropriate it was for this ecumenical initiative to be taken by an ex-SCM secretary and a member of the SSM. In a couple of cyclostyled memos outlining the origins and purpose of the Week of Prayer, Gabriel tells how the Week was first observed in Australia, and pays tribute to the particular contribution of the SCM:

> 'If we look back over 50 years, one of the outstanding things is the immense influence which the Student Christian Movement has exercised in the movement towards Christian Unity; it has trained those who today are the leaders. Thus has arisen Faith and Order, Life and Work and now the World Council of Churches, which issues annually its Call to Prayer for Unity.
>
> The fact that we in Australia are going back from the January date to Ascensiontide is solely due to our climate; January is not a fit month at least in the southern parts of Australia. In 1954 Ormond College, Melbourne, and St Michael's House, Crafers, S.A., agreed to keep it together. In 1955 there were committees of the Week of Prayer at Melbourne, Adelaide and Brisbane ... At Melbourne and Adelaide prayer was made in some selected city churches during the lunch-hour on weekdays. At Melbourne there was an excellent meeting in the university, under the auspices of the Newman Society, the Australian SCM, and the Evangelical Union'.[8]

Australia put Gabriel at the furthest possible distance from the college and community at Kelham, but the significant consequence of this geographical distance was that it enabled him to see himself and his relationships with the English brethren in a new perspective. On Easter Day 1953, in a letter to the Director, Gabriel told how Basil Oddie, the Fr Provincial at St Michael's House, had helped him to face things in himself and had confronted him with the need to repair the strained relationships which he had with some of the brethren at Kelham. In a disarmingly honest and perceptive latter, Gabriel made this confession:

> 'I believe he (Basil) has told you about the bash that he gave me just over a week ago, telling me things about myself, some of which I was half aware of, and some not. I am immensely grateful, for it threw a new light on a lot of things in my life at Kelham, and on the root of it all in the love of the ego, as though I was Somebody and as though my ideas and insights etc. were Mine. I did not realise before that my departure from Kelham was for Kelham's good: but so it was'.

From this attitude of penitence sprang a greater willingness to respond to the opportunities which were to come his way. It was as if this difficult business of facing himself somehow released greater energies and zest for life, for although he was entering his late sixties, Gabriel became increasingly involved and committed to serving the needs of the Church in Australia. To some extent this was aided by his willingness to continue thinking and to develop theologically. Prompted by Davis McCaughey he re-read and re-evaluated his views on Rudolf Bultmann, and was generally delighted to discover new authors and insights. In 1958 he even polished his German, so that he could read Gunther Bornkamm, a theologian with whom he was much taken, and with whom he subsequently corresponded. (In the late 1960s, when Bornkamm was conducting a lecture tour in Australia, he asked if he could visit St Michael's House on account of Gabriel's association with the place). Gabriel continued to think, to write and to teach, and his *God's Kingdom and Ours* (SCM, 1959) is the best distillation of his thinking in the related areas of mission and ecumenism. Besides his writing and his teaching commitments in the college, he was often invited to preach and lecture, not only in Adelaide, but also in Melbourne and in Sydney. In Sydney he managed to gain the confidence and trust of some of the most partisan Anglican evangelicals, and this certainly opened up, as we shall see in the final chapter, a whole cluster of questions surrounding the question of the authority of scripture.

By the time Gabriel was called back to Kelham in 1961, he was well rooted in Australia with a wide range of contacts, and esteemed by a number of colleagues from a variety of ecclesial traditions. The return to England was certainly a wrench for him and for his Australian friends, not least the McCaughey family. His final contribution to church life in Australia was to act as a theological consultant for the joint Commission of the Australian Congregational, Methodist and Presbyterian churches, which began a process which eventually resulted with the inauguration of the Uniting Church in Australia on 22 June 1977. His years in Australia certainly vindicate Gabriel's reputation of being an ecumenical pioneer, but the story of his efforts in this sphere needs to be told in greater detail.

2
THE SCANDINAVIAN
CONNECTION

THIS ACCOUNT of Gabriel's Scandinavian connection begins not with its origins, but at a particularly poignant moment in the story. In July 1931, Gabriel, together with two other British delegates to the Anglo-Scandinavian Theological Conference, and Professor Nörregaard of Copenhagen, were staying at Archbishop Söderblom's house in Uppsala. Söderblom had taken a personal interest in the conference, and had helped with some of the planning. Unfortunately, other commitments had made it impossible for him to participate fully in the conference, but he did manage to attend the final day. This was to be the last day of his working life. The following day he was taken into hospital and died on 12 July. The visitors staying at the Archbishop's house were stunned and saddened, but Yngve Brilioth, Söderblom's son-in-law, insisted on taking them on a little trip, which had been suggested a few days earlier by Söderblom himself. Brilioth took the small party of visitors over to the little island of Björkö, the reputed site of one of the earliest Christian missions. St Anskar, a Frankish Benedictine monk, had established a Christian mission on the island in AD 829, and the achievement of this missionary monk had caught the imagination of the young Söderblom, who at the age of twenty-three, wrote a small booklet on Anskar and the planting of Christianity on Swedish soil. In the summer of 1930, Söderblom dedicated a new chapel on the island of Bjökö, built at his suggestion to commemorate the 1,100th anniversary of Anskar's mission.

So, in Gabriel's mind, Brilioth's trip to the island of Bjökö on Lake Mälaren, was a memorable visit, and 'a true pilgrimage of Anskar and of Nathan Söderblom'. The details of the visit were movingly recounted in a letter which Gabriel wrote to his mother, on 15 July, when he was literally on the North Sea, on his return passage to England. In this letter, he pays the following tribute to Söderblom: '. . . he was perhaps the greatest Christian leader at the time of his

death, and the greatest name in the whole history of the Swedish
Church. The work he has done for the Swedish Church cannot be
measured. All the younger leaders of the Swedish Church today are
his disciples'. Other tributes were soon to follow. For English readers,
an account of Söderblom's thought and theological writing, written
by Gustav Aulén, and translated by Gabriel, appeared in the *Church
Quarterly Review*, (CQR, October 1932). The following year, at Mrs
Söderblom's request, Gabriel's translation of some of Soderblom's
sermons on the Passion of of Christ were published, with the English
title, *The Mystery of the Cross* (SCM, 1933). Although Gabriel was
not entirely satisfied with his English translation, it did enable the
English reader to discover something of the profundity of Soderblom's spirituality, and put into their hands 'a little book of rare distinction'.

The Great Archbishop

Nathan Söderblom, (1866–1931), the son of a Swedish priest, had
been brought up in an atmosphere of nineteenth-century Lutheran
piety in the manse at Trönö, in Hälsingland. As a young man he
became a serious and able scholar, and without losing a sense of
loyalty to the traditions in which he had been nurtured as a Christian,
he began to develop a critical interest in the origins of Lutheranism.
Eventually he became an authority on the German Reformer, Martin
Luther. He lectured extensively, and in 1919 published *Humour and
Melancholy in Martin Luther*. As the title indicates, Söderblom was
fascinated by Luther's religious psychology; he maintained that
Luther needed to be seen in the context of Catholic thought and
practice, and in his portrait of the Reformer, Söderblom showed a
high degree of continuity between Luther the Catholic and Luther
the Protestant. Besides this particular interest in Luther, Söderblom's
other scholarly activity centred around the History of Religions, and
it was in the field of the comparative study of religions that his real
expertise lay. His research in this field led him to recognise truth in
non-Christian religions, and to emphasise the sovereign freedom of
God. He believed that the transcendent God communicated with
humanity in different epochs and in different ways, and that such
revelation could not be equivocally identified with any single human
writing, or form of religious experience. A view such as this would
have been acceptable to the true disciple of the theological maverick,
Herbert Kelly.

Söderblom's academic career was meteoric. At the age of thirty-five, he was given a professorial chair in the University of Uppsala, and eleven years later, in 1912, he became Professor of the History of Religion at Leipzig, in Germany. This appointment, however, was soon curtailed. In 1914, as war was breaking out, Söderblom was elected to be Archbishop of Uppsala. The archepiscopal consecration was a most splendid occasion, and took place on 8 November, a date of his own choosing, which happened to be the date of his father's birthday. His return to Sweden was a positive return to the Church which had nurtured his Christian life and outlook, but Söderblom realised too that he was returning to a country which was isolated from the main stream of European life.

Archbishop Söderblom was tireless, and at time's impetuous, in his endeavours to call Christians from various traditions to a wider vision, but the need was urgent as Europe became the theatre of a most disastrous war. The world needed to hear Christ's word of peace, and to see the different churches working together across denominational and national barriers. Certain opportunities presented themselves when hostilities came to an end, but even then, international relations were tense with suspicion and recrimination. Söderblom supported organisations such as the World Alliance, which sought to restore the social fabric of a war-torn Europe and lay foundations for a lasting peace, but he was even more anxious to mobilise the churches as agents of reconciliation and practical help and relief. After extensive negotiations, and a series of planning committees, it began to look as if his hopes might be realised, or at least launched, with the proposed 'Life and Work' Conference to be held in Stockholm in 1925.

Söderblom's call to the churches was motivated by the need of healing and reconstruction in Europe, and this pragmatic imperative was enhanced by a particular vision of the Church, which he called 'evangelical catholicity'. What Soderblom envisaged was not a mono-lithic and uniform ecclesiastical structure, or some pan-Protestant organisation, but a movement which would permeate and encompass all the churches, for the sake of the Gospel and the Church's effective service to, and within, the world at large. It was to be a movement which was decidedly evangelistic, and universal, and which would show in the life and worship of the various churches, the 'variety in unity' of Christian witness.

Söderblom's 'evangelical catholicity' stood very close to Fr Kelly's notion of catholicity. In Kelly's writings the notion is elusive, but firmly grounded in the view that God's dealings with humanity are universal and inclusive. So, to speak of the Church as being catholic, is to use the term in a secondary and derivative sense. Having learnt from both Fr Kelly and Söderblom, Gabriel, in his last book, could argue that the true catholic is also evangelical.[1]

Stockholm 1925

The 'Universal Christian Conference on Life and Work' drew some six hundred delegates to Stockholm. It began on 19 August, and worked through a rather overcrowded agenda until 30 August. The conference was a significant meeting at various levels. It was a meeting between those who had formerly been enemies, a meeting between the old world of Europe and the new world of the United States, and a meeting across denominational boundaries, with delegates representing the Reformed, Lutheran, Anglican, Methodist and Orthodox churches. The most colourful and sartorially conspicuous contingent were the Orthodox delegates, led by Photios, Patriarch of Alexandria, and Germanos, Metropolitan of Thyateira. Rome had refused to attend, and this was a cause of deep disappointment for Söderblom, who had made frequent attempts to secure the participation of Roman Catholics. He was all too conscious of Rome's absence, and this led him to make what is probably one of the best remembered sayings of the whole conference: 'Two men are here gathered together. John the apostle of tender love and contemplation, and Paul the greatest disciple of the Saviour ... The third man, Peter, the spokeman of the disciples, still tarries. Christendom stands out as divided, but Christ is One'.

Among the Anglican delegates at the conference was an accomplished and distinguished priest, in early middle years, Fr Reginald Tribe SSM, who two months earlier, on 17 June, had been elected Director of the Society by its Great Chapter meeting at Kelham. Fr Tribe shared Söderblom's ecumenical outlook and his concern with social questions, and came to espouse the 'Life and Work' movement which he inspired. Some years later, Fr Tribe became a prominent member of the British Council of Churches, and as well as his commitment to Christian social action, he also became involved in the other side of the ecumenical coin, the 'Faith and Order' movement. Geoffrey Curtis, of the Community of the Resurrection, has described Fr Tribe as one of the martyrs of the ecumenical movement, because he was tragically killed by a German bomb in London, when he was attending a meeting of the Faith and Order Commission in 1943.

Anglican–Swedish Relations

Relations between the Church of England and the Church of Sweden had been developing over a considerable number of years. As early as 1888, the Lambeth Conference had resolved that 'approaches on the part of the Swedish Church, with a view to mutual explanations of differences, be most gladly welcomed, in order to move towards the ultimate establishment, if possible, of intercommunion on sound principles of ecclesiastical polity'. In 1908, the Swedish Bishop of Kalmar, Bishop Tottie, was an official visitor to the Lambeth Conference, and presented a letter from Archbishop Ekman of Uppsala, which suggested the opening of formal conversations and dialogue between the two churches. This initiative was welcomed by the Lambeth Fathers, and an official commission was appointed to enter into dialogue with the Church of Sweden. The commission consisted of three Anglican bishops, Ryle, Wordsworth, and Williams, and two academics, A.J.Mason and E.R.Bernard. The commission visited Uppsala the following year, 1909, and submitted its report in 1911. The report was substantially positive and made the following statements concerning the ministry of the Church of Sweden:

1 The succession of bishops had been maintained unbroken, and that it had a true conception of the episcopal office
2 The office of priest was also rightly conceived as a divinely appointed instrument for the ministry of word and sacraments, and that it had been in intention handed on throughout the whole history of the Church of Sweden.

Alongside these affirmations of the Church of Sweden's ministerial orders, observations were also made of those features of the Church's ministry which did not comply with the practice of the Church of England. The understanding and exercise of the diaconate, the first of the threefold orders of ministry, and the practice of confirmation, were two cases in point.

Up until the seventeenth century, the diaconate in the Church of Sweden, as elsewhere in the west, had been regarded as being preparatory to the priesthood. However, with the gradual assimilation of the Lutheran conception of the diaconate as being a ministry of pastoral care, the Swedish Church came to adopt a permanent diaconate. Deacons were episcopally ordained, but were generally reckoned as not belonging to the ranks of the clergy. During his first visit to Sweden in 1928, Gabriel soon came to hold the opinion that there was much that the Anglican Church could usefully learn from this practice of the permanent diaconate. Gabriel felt that the proper pastoral role of the deacon needed to be balanced with a distinct and proper liturgical role, and he ventured to make the point in a private conversation with Bishop Rodhe of Lund. The bishop was definite in his repudiation of the view that the deacon should serve at the Lord's table in the sanctuary: 'No; and it is not expedient, because the people would misunderstand it'. Needless to say, the question of the liturgical role of the deacon became an important issue for the emerging 'high-church party' within the Church of Sweden.

To return to the Commission's report of 1911, the second area of difficulty was the practice of confirmation in the Swedish Church. In the Church of Sweden, confirmation was regarded solely in terms of admission to communion, and was administered by the parish priest. The rite did not even contain a laying-on of hands, so even a vestige of a sacramental celebration was lacking. In the Church of England, the rite of confirmation, then as now, was jealously guarded by the bishops, and this aspect of Christian initiation continues to be a live issue in discussion between the two churches.

Archbishop Söderblom was irritated by the fact that the Commissioners had highlighted confirmation as a possible sticking point in relations between the two churches. In practice, the Swedish Church had been the first to offer eucharistic hospitality, and in Söderblom's mind, this gesture represented a tacit recognition of the Anglican rite of confirmation. Furthermore, in terms of Swedish practice, confirmation marked the culmination of a thorough process of Christian formation and instruction, which compared favourably with the rather perfunctory preparation which invariably preceeded the celebration of the Anglican rite of confirmation. Even today, preparation for confirmation in the Swedish Church extends over a whole year, and a variety of teaching methods and learning opportunities will be employed.

The early conversations and official discussions between the two churches were seriously disrupted by the disastrous 1914–18 war, and the Commissioners' report of 1911 was not formally received by the Lambeth bishops until the Lambeth Conference of 1920. This Conference was certainly one of the most momentous of the Lambeth Conferences. The Conference was fired with an extraordinary ecumenical vision and issued a historic appeal for the reunion of all

Christian peoples. The appeal took the form of an open letter, and being addressed to 'all Christian people', was addressed to the widest possible Christian constituency. The inclusivity of this appeal was matched with a truly catholic understanding of Christian faith to produce what must certainly be considered to be one of the most profound statements on the nature of Christian unity. 'The vision which rises before us is that of a Church genuinely Catholic, loyal to all Truth, and gathering into its fellowship all who profess and call themselves Christians, within whose visible unity and order, bequeathed as a heritage by the past to the present, shall be possessed in common and made servicable to the whole Body of Christ. Within this unity Christian Communions now separated from one another would retain much that has long been distinctive in their methods of worship and service. It is through a rich diversity of life and devotion that the unity of the whole fellowship will be fulfilled'.[2]

In 1920 the Lambeth Fathers resolved that 'members of the Swedish Church qualified to receive the sacrament in their own church, should be admitted to Holy Communion in ours'. This opening of intercommunion between the two churches was strengthened by a statement which amounted to a mutual recognition of ministries, recommending that 'in the event of an invitation to an Anglican bishop, or bishops, to take part in the consecration of a Swedish bishop, it might properly be accepted'. Söderblom, in fact, had already written privately to Hensley Henson inviting him to take part in the consecration of two Swedish bishops at Uppsala Cathedral in September 1920. In the event, two Anglican bishops, Hensley Henson and Theodore Woods, the Bishop of Peterborough, took part in the Swedish consecrations. However, it was some seven years before a Swedish bishop took part in the consecration of an Anglican bishop.

Throughout this intensive period of official conversations and exchanges between the two churches, the Archbishop of Canterbury, Randall Davidson, appeared to stand a little aloof, and perhaps he was a little too satisfied with the liberal and comprehensive catholicism which he believed was well represented by mainstream Anglicanism. Söderblom found Randall Davidson's attitude a little too complacent and smug, but that did not cool his own ardour. Indeed, he welcomed the initiatives of the Lambeth Fathers with alacrity, and in a judicious letter, composed jointly with his trusted and able friends, Bishop Billing of Västera·s, and Professor K.B.Westman, and which formed the official answer from the Swedish Bishops' Conference, the possible basis for a more formal relationship between the two churches was set in place.

However, not everyone shared Soderblom's enthusiasm for a closer relationship between the Church of Sweden and the Church of England. In Sweden, the old conservative Bishop of Göteborg, E.H.Rodhe, sounded a note of caution and warned that too close a relationship with the Church of England might strain their existing relationships with sister Lutheran churches, particularly the Lutheran Church in Germany. In England, a considerable degree of disquiet over the relationship between the two churches was voiced in certain Anglo-Catholic circles. An editorial article in the *Church Times*, for instance, questioned the pedigree of the Swedish 'apostolic succession', and in a rather superior vein argued that intercommunion with the Church of Sweden would compromise the Church of England's catholic status and standing.

Come over and see!

On 2 November 1927, Fredrick Kjellander, the parish priest of Stenstorp, in Sweden, wrote to Fr Reginald Tribe, reminding him that they had met briefly in Stockholm at the time of the 'ecumenical council'. In this letter Kjellanger laments the fact that a number of articles and letters published in the *Church Times* could easily thwart the cause of ecumenism and frustrate the relationship between the Church of England and the Church of Sweden, and asks whether a young and able Anglo-Catholic priest might visit Sweden in order to gain some first hand knowledge of what the Church of Sweden really was. Kjellander's invitation offered hospitality and 'free lessons in the Swedish language'. Fr Tribe responded positively, and because Gabriel had shown a considerable flair in learning other languages during his time in South Africa, it was decided that Gabriel should visit Sweden on a 'fact finding tour' the following summer.

The SSM already had some links with Scandinavia, and Gabriel's planned visit in August 1928 was seen as a way of extending those links. The first connection the SSM had with Scandinavia was a link with Denmark, which had been made two years previously in 1926. Many years later, Gabriel wrote an account of this original Scandinavian connection in an article in the SSM Quarterly. The article tells of a theological student from Copenhagen who had spent a week at Kelham in 1926, and how the student was impressed by the fact that 'while Copenhagen University provided them with studies only, men at Kelham had not only studies, but also a common liturgical life in the chapel, a common social and domestic life, and pastoral care'. The student referred to here was Thomas Lonborg-Jensen, and what had clearly impressed him at Kelham was a holistic vision of the theological enterprise, with academic study being integrated with the life of a praying community. On his return to Copenhagen, Thomas was determined 'to bring together a group of students who would, as far as possible, try to do these things for themselves'.

For Thomas Lonborg-Jensen, the hope of establishing some form of community life for theological students was no wish-dream, and resulted in the Theologisk Oratorium, a society which was flourishing when Gabriel made his final visit to Scandinavia in June 1961. Today, the Oratorium has attracted a number of priests of a more conservative attitude, many of whom contributed to the new liturgy, and its real value is in providing a network of contacts and support for those with a more catholic and ecumenical approach to the worship and mission of the Danish Church.

Gabriel embarked on his first visit to Sweden on 8 August 1928, and arrived at Malmö on 11 August. There he was met by the vicar of Malmö, St Peter's, Albert Lysander. Initially, Gabriel felt rather self-conscious walking around the city wearing his habit, for as he recorded in his diary, 'people stare as I have never seen people stare before'. A few days later, when Gabriel was being shown the market town of Skara, someone asked Gabriel's companion who the habited figure was. 'The pope' was the reply, and the man apparently walked away, saying, 'Lord, have mercy upon us'. There was, as this incident shows, considerable suspicion, ignorance, and hostility towards the Roman Catholic Church, and religious, both monks and nuns, were at that time unknown in the Church of Sweden. Historically, the Order of St Bridget, originally a twin monastery, which had been founded by that extraordinary women, St Birgitta, in 1346, at Vadstena, on Lake Vattern, survived for some seventy years after the Reformation in Sweden. By the end of the sixteenth century the religious life in the Swedish Church had come to an end, and it was not until the 1930s that a little interest in the religious life began to be shown. The first religious community to come into being since the Reformation was a women's community, the Order of the Holy Spirit, and the first sister made her religious profession in 1954. Since then a number of communities have been founded, but as there is so little tradition of religious life in the Church of Sweden, there has been little to sustain them, and consequently, most have remained

very small with only three or four sisters. Some religious have
become Roman Catholics, and in one case, a whole community of
Franciscan brothers became Roman Catholic. Today, the only surviv-
ing men's community is the Brotherhood of the Holy Cross, founded
in the 1960s, at Östänback, which is a Benedictine house of twelve
monks. An Anglican link with this community has recently been
renewed by the Community of the Resurrection, at Mirfield.

On his first visit to Sweden, Gabriel was impressed with the
generous and warm hospitality of the Swedes. He came to enjoy their
food, and soon adjusted to their natural and uninhibited attitude to
life. Such an attitude showed itself when Gabriel joined a family
swimming excursion to Lake Vänern, and 'nobody minded in the
least having neither costumes, nor towels'. The Swedish attitude was
natural and good, and Gabriel found the country a most congenial
place. In a letter to Fr Tribe, written during a subsequent visit,
Gabriel was able to say 'It is remarkable how when one comes to
Sweden one feels immediately a more spacious atmosphere and at
home'.

The aim of Gabriel's first visit to Sweden was not only to acclimatise himself and become more proficient in the language, but also to
make personal contacts, and to contribute in some small way to the
dialogue between the two churches. To this end, Kjellander had
arranged a small three-day conference, which would involve six
Swedish priests, three deacons and a theological student. It was
arranged for Gabriel to read a paper on each of the three days. The
first paper sought to give an account of the strengths and weaknesses
of the Anglo-Catholic movement. This was a balanced and critical
paper. He spoke positively of the need of the Church to challenge the
rather bland attitude of nominal Christianity, which all too often
afflicts a national church, and recorded the most significant achievement of Anglo-Catholicism, which was to recall the Church of
England to the sacramental basis of its life and worship. At this point
in the paper, Gabriel spoke of the desirability of having a weekly
communicating Parish Eucharist as the chief Sunday service, a point
which shows that his mind was already working along the the lines
of a 'Parish Communion'.

In this first paper Gabriel did not shrink from offering some
stringent criticisms of the Anglo-Catholic movement. The most
serious weakness of the movement was its encouragement of a party-
spirit. Such a partisan attitude, Gabriel argued, contradicted the very
claim which those who were so anxious to be called 'catholic' were

wanting to make. The implications of this point were drawn out in Gabriel's second paper, entitled, 'Catholicism'. The main line of argument in this paper proposed that the essence of catholicism for a national church, like the Church of England, and the Church of Sweden, was a living sense of being a part of the universal Church. In connection with this point, Gabriel raised some interesting questions about continuity and change in the history of the church and suggested that tradition, which he described as the vital life-blood of the Church catholic, was not to be confused with conservatism, or the kind of romanticism which seeks to preserve an all too often imagined past.

Gabriel's third paper was concerned with theological education and gave an account of the aims and methods of theological study which were followed at Kelham. Christian theology, he claimed, had to engage the whole person, and in the final analysis was concerned with the theological formation of the person, the inculcation of a theological sense, and not the acquisition of doctrinal correctitude. Study, he said, 'cannot be separated from life', and to illustrate the point he said that when a student came to study the doctrine of justification, he must 'find the meaning of it in life, in his own life, and in his prayers'. Here was no abstract academic theology, but a lived and prayed theology which had to be approached with the utmost intellectual rigour. This view of theological study as theological formation was well received by Gabriel's new Swedish friends, but communication was not particularly easy. In fact all three papers were delivered in English and Kjellander had to translate every sentence as Gabriel spoke.

On 4 September Gabriel caught the ferry at Malmö and sailed over to Denmark, where he conducted a quiet day at Sölleröd, which had been arranged for the eight members of Thomas Jensen's Oratory. The participants, it seems, were unused to keeping silent retreats and quiet days, but nevertheless the day was worthwhile and strengthened Gabriel's links with the embryonic Theologisk Oratorium. From Denmark, Gabriel sailed back to England, and returned to Kelham with a deeper understanding of the Scandinavian churches and a new found love for Nordic Christianity.

From his first Scandinavian visit in 1928, Gabriel's contacts with members of the Swedish and the Danish church widened considerably. As we have seen, by 1931 he was an official delegate of the Anglo-Scandinavian Theological Conference, the second of its kind, which was led on the Anglican side by the Bishop of Middleton, the

Rt Revd Geoffrey Parsons. The purpose of these biennial conferences was primarily for theological exchange. Gabriel, along with Leslie Hunter and Alan Richardson, was a frequent delegate, and on his return from Australia, Gabriel received a letter from Geoffrey Lampe inviting him 'to rejoin the party'. Apart from these formal meetings between theologians, Gabriel also became involved in promoting wider contacts between Anglicans and the Nordic churches. After the Second World War, for instance, he became a prominent member of the Anglican Swedish Church Association, whose task was to facilitate exchanges between the two churches. Despite his innate awkwardness, Gabriel had a natural gift for making friends, and largely through correspondence was diligent in maintaining his friendships. A good example of a Scandinavian relationship was his friendship with Regin Prenter, which lasted for thirty years until Gabriel died. Prenter was one of the founding members of the Danish Theologisk Oratorium, and had attended the quiet day led by Gabriel at Sollerod, in 1928. The following summer, Prenter was among a party of nine Danes who came over to England to attend an SCM Conference at Swanwick, and then spent a week at Kelham. At Kelham the Danish party took a full part in the liturgical life of the community and heard Fr Kelly lecture. Gabriel recognised the potential of Regin Prenter and encouraged him in his aspirations to become a theologian. In 1935–6 Regin spent a year at Lincoln Theological College, where he came under the influence of Michael Ramsey, who was then chaplain and tutor at the college. From Lincoln, Prenter was able to make frequent visits to Kelham and to meet and talk with Gabriel who became a mentor to the young theologian. In 1958, after an interval of twenty-two years, Regin Prenter was able to spend a little time at Kelham, and during this visit he wrote to Gabriel, who was then at St Michael's House, Crafers, South Australia, saying that his visit to Kelham was a 'coming home after a long journey'. Regin Prenter, who died in 1990, had a distinguished career as a systematic theologian, and with the publication of *Spiritus Creator*, (1944) sealed his reputation as a Luther scholar. As Professor of Dogmatics in the University of Åarhus, in Denmark, and a visiting lecturer in the University of Strasbourg, Regin Prenter was a professional theologian, but unlike some of his contemporary counterparts, he recognised that the *prima theologica* was the business of the worshipping community, such as he had experienced in the Great Chapel at Kelham.

The Swedish Church – Catholic and Reformed

The more familiar Gabriel became with the Church of Sweden, the more he saw a close correspondence between its history, ethos and liturgical forms, and that of the Church of England. Thus when he came to give an account of the English Reformation in his *Liturgy and Society* (Faber, 1935) Gabriel claimed that the nearest parallel to the English Reformation in the west was the Church of Sweden.

Historically speaking, the Reformation in Sweden had been moderate and gradual, and as was the case in England, it had been political change which had precipitated religious reform. From the fourteenth century, the Scandinavian countries had formed a confederacy of the three states of Denmark, Norway and Sweden, called the Kalmar union, ruled by one monarch. At various times particular states jostled for positions of supremacy, and in January 1520, Sweden again claimed its independence. Christian II, the last in the line of the union kings, attempted to suppress the Swedish rebellion, on the pretext of strengthening the Church's power and influence. His intention of subjugating the Swedish people was not uncontested, and he was soon resisted by a popular leader, Gustavus Vasa. Vasa succeeded in mobilising support for his campaign against the unpopular Christian II, and thereby united the nobility and the peasantry. With his forces Vasa effectively broke the power of Christian II and his close ally Archbishop Gustaf Trolle, and within the year the king was deposed and fled to Wittenberg, finally being imprisoned in a castle in South Jutland. He died a prisoner in Denmark. With his removal from the scene, the ground was clear for Sweden to emerge as an independent state, and Gustavus Vasa seized the opportunity. His immediate task was to consolidate his own power-base by securing financial support, and in order to achieve both financial support and popular acclaim, he was compelled to loosen Rome's hold over the country. The Pope foolishly supported the Swedish Archbishop Trolle and thereby miscalculated the situation. Gustavus Vasa had a broad support base and was waiting for an opportunity to challenge Rome. The decisive time came in 1523, when the Swedish Church required three more bishops. Vasa requested a dispensation from the customary fees required by the Pope for the electoral confirmation and consecration of new bishops, and threatened that if the dispensation was not granted by the Curia, then he would assume Rome's prerogative and himself confirm the election of the new bishops. The Curia refused to issue a dispensation, and what transpired was a muddled and compromised situation in which only one episcopal candidate, Petrus Magni, was confirmed by the Pope as Bishop of Västerås, and consecrated in Rome. Petrus Magni then officiated as consecrator of the new bishops in Sweden, thereby safeguarding the apostolic succession in the Church of Sweden.

Meanwhile, Gustavus Vasa had recruited a literate and cultured young man, Olavus Petri, to be the city clerk in Stockholm. Olavus Petri had studied at Wittenberg between 1516 and 1518, and had been impressed by the German Reformer, Martin Luther, and sympathetically viewed his programme of religious reform. Thus he came to share Luther's deep conviction that the Bible should be translated into the vernacular language of the people, and in 1526 Olavus Petri published a Swedish translation of the New Testament.

The following year, at the Diet of Västerås, which had been convened by Gustavus Vasa, the fate of the Swedish Church was sealed. The country was on the verge of bankruptcy and the most immediate solution was to siphon money from the Church to the State coffers, and to confiscate what Gustavus and his associates considered to be superfluous and opulent episcopal and monastic property. At this suggestion the bishops were outraged and Gustavus wavered, but in the end, his hand was strengthened by the nobility and he was able to seize money and real estate from the Church. From that point onwards, the State would effectively administer the Church, and her clergy were no longer excempt from the civil courts, and were obliged to preach the Word and to read the Bible in the vernacular in churches and schools. In this way, the Reformation emphasis upon preaching, and its attendent theology of the Word, was written into the law of the land, and the ability to preach soon became a condition of ordination to the priesthood. Religiously the tide had turned, and Archbishop Trolle and his loyal supporter, the Bishop of Linköping, the second most senior bishop in Sweden, were living in exile.

On 12 January 1528, Gustavus Vasa was anointed and crowned King of Sweden by the Bishop of Skara, according to the full traditional catholic rites, and on that splendid occasion Olavus Petri preached the sermon. The occasion marked with due ceremony the emergence of Sweden as an independent State, and its Church as a reformed catholic church, thereby marking the final break with Rome. In 1531 Olavus Petri's brother, Laurentius Petri was appointed Archbishop of Uppsala, and a new chapter in the history of the

Swedish Church began. For a number of years the Church of Sweden oscillated between being a catholic and a protestant institution, but the decisive step, effectively halting any tendency towards a Calvinistic character, was taken at the Synod of Uppsala in March 1593. This synod formally adopted the Augsburg Confession, an eirenical Lutheran document, which had been penned by Melancthon in 1530, and which asserted the primacy of scripture, and its status of being the final arbiter of true Christian life and doctrine.

The abiding significance of the Uppsala Synod of 1593, and its implications regarding the status of the Swedish Church, was set out by Gabriel in an essay on the Scandinavian Communions, which was published as part of a series of studies on other churches produced by the Church Union in 1940. In this essay Gabriel argues that '. . . 1593 is the terminal point of the Swedish Reformation . . . they went back to Laurentius Petri and his *Church Order*, and accepted for the first time officially, a Lutheran formula: the Augsburg Confession. To this day the word "Lutheran" does not form part of the official name of the Church of Sweden; it is simply Svenska Kyrkan'.[3] Unsurprisingly, it is with some satisfaction that Gabriel was able to assert that throughout the Reformation period of its history, the Church of Sweden remained an episcopal church.

Gabriel's essay gave a comprehensive survey of the history, character and liturgy of the Scandinavian churches, and a most positive estimate of the Church of Sweden to the Anglo-Catholic constituency of the Church of England. Much of what was written there, of course, was gleaned from what he had learnt on his visits to the country, and it is to his first visit in August 1928 that we must now return.

Worship in the Church of Sweden

All that Gabriel saw, his impressions, and conversations were carefully recorded in his 'Logbook of Visit to Sweden and Denmark, 1928'. As a personal diary, or travelogue, it is full of human interest, but a particular feature is the detailed descriptions of the religious services which he attended. Here indeed, we see a man with a keen fascination for matters liturgical. A good example of this is his account of a visit to the church of St Peter, Malmö, a rather splendid fourteenth century Gothic building, with a very fine and ornate altar and reredos of seventeenth-century Danish work, with a prominent pulpit in the same style, thus exhibiting an equal emphasis upon

Word and Sacrament. What Gabriel describes here, is an evening celebration of the Eucharist, using the 1917 revision of the Swedish mass, which curiously, seems to have been concelebrated:

'The service begins with the Skriftermal, the Preparation. The communicants, about thirty, were grouped in the front of the nave and opposite the altar. The priest arrived in alb and stole, and after a hymn gave an address of fifteen to twenty minutes from the altar. Then followed some prayers of confession and absolution after which the priest returned to the vestry. The assistant priest, who had been sitting in the vicarage pew with his wife, also went into the vestry. Soon they both appeared in green chasubles, approaching the altar from either side, and stood side by side at the altar, so that one could see the sacred vessels between them. The Eucharist proper began with the sursum corda, followed by the Preface and the recital of the Institution narrative, and the Our Father. The parish priest (the kyrkoherde) took the greater part, but the Lord's Prayer was said by the assistant priest. The sanctus, immediately after the Lord's Prayer, was sung by the choir, which was followed by "the peace of the Lord be always with you." Then the communicants approached and knelt at the rails, and while the Agnes dei was sung, the two priests stood facing them holding the sacred elements. After the railful had been communicated, the assistant priest gave the kyrkeherd his communion, and then dismissed the people. After the second railful had been communicated, the assistant priest similarly received. Then a prayer of thanksgiving and an act of praise, and the blessing concluded the service.

It was a memorable sight ... the lights, the people kneeling and the two men in vestments standing before them holding the sacred elements. It had a dignity and a solemnity of its own: I have never seen quite the same in the Anglican Church, or the Roman. It was slow and unhurried, with no fussiness whatever'.

The eucharistic rite which would have been used on that memorable occasion would have been ostensibly that which had been introduced by the Swedish Reformer, Olavus Petri, but what had so forcefully communicated itself to Gabriel on that occasion was something of the mystery of the eucharistic presence; that element of eucharistic experience which even so radical a reformer as Martin

Luther consciously affirmed and sought to preserve in his own liturgical rites.

Gabriel's description of the evening celebration of the Swedish mass, at St Peter's, Malmo, manages to capture and highlight some of the salient features of the Swedish liturgy. The first of these features is what we might describe as the catholic ambience of the celebration; the second, the prominence of prayers of preparation and confession, and thirdly, the act of Communion itself. To help fill in the background to Gabriel's description, we might comment on these three features in turn.

First, the catholic ambience. A great number of churches in Sweden had been built in the Middle Ages, and because there had never been a period of iconoclasm, such, for instance, as was known in England during the time of the Puritan ascendency, a great deal of church decoration and religious art remained. During the time of reformation only the side altars were removed, (because of their association with private and votive masses), but in most churches the elaborate and finely crafted reredoses, crucifixes, stained glass, and candle holders were left intact. So, at least in visual terms, in terms of what struck the eye of a person entering a church building, the impression given would have been the impression of a catholic setting for worship. Such a perception, of course, would have suggested that the Swedish Reformation was, at least liturgically speaking, a conservative Reformation.

In fact, the first tentative steps in the reform of the eucharistic liturgy were taken by Olavus Petri, (1493–1552), who produced a vernacular Order for Communion in 1531. In this project he was influenced by Luther's *Formula Missae et Communionis* (1523), originally drafted for use at the church at Wittenberg, Petri extended Luther's Preface to provide an economically expressed recital of the Christ-event as a prelude to the so-called words of Institution. The sanctus, following Luther's arrangement, was placed, without any linking phrase, between the Institution narrative and the Lord's Prayer. An exhortation, a real hall-mark of Reformed liturgy, was insinuated between the Agnes dei and the administration of Communion. Again, as with Luther, certain medieval customs, such as the elevation of the elements after the dominical words in the Institution narrative were retained. The retention of vestments and some of the old ritual would certainly have signalled an element of continuity between the Latin and the Swedish Mass. Interestingly, Petri continued to use the term mass for the Eucharist, and no attempt was made to impose the vernacular rite upon the church, and it seems that in many parts of the country, the Latin mass continued for some considerable time.

Laurentius Petri, Olavus' brother, continued the task of liturgical reform, and produced some four revisions of the Swedish Mass. In 1531 he became the Archbishop of Uppsala, and his most significant and enduring work was the compilation of a 'Church Order' in 1571. This provided the Church of Sweden with a kind of constitutional document. Among other things, it limited the sovereign's power over the church, and preserved the accoutrements of catholic eucharistic worship. As the Order declares 'elevations, mass vestments, altars, altar clothes, lights, and whatsoever of these ceremonies have been adopted, . . . may we freely attain as optional matters'.

The second feature of the Swedish mass which invites further comment is the importance attached to the preparation and the prayer of confession.

In Germany, Luther had admonished the faithful to participate frequently in the mass, and demanded that they should receive Communion in both kinds, the chalice as well as the host. In Sweden, Olavus Petri had the same agenda, and sought to promote a regular weekly Communion for the faithful. Both Reformers believed that the act of Communion required a deliberate and conscious preparation on the part of the intending communicant. In Sweden a form of public self-examination and confession was compiled to facilitate such preparation. Originally the form was used in church on the Saturday evening, and all those who were intending to receive Communion on the Sunday were expected to attend. Eventually a form of preparation was compiled to be used immediately before the celebration of the sacrament. This was the Skriftermål mentioned by Gabriel. Originally the Skriftermål consisted of two hymns, one at the beginning and the other at the end, a reading and exposition of the Word, (which according to the Lutheran scheme of things, was intended to drive the faithful to repentence and to impress upon them their dependence upon the divine mercy and grace), and an absolution, the declaration of God's forgiveness. The Skriftermål became appended to the mass, the Högmässa, which itself included a prayer of confession and absolution, and so the whole service was considerably weighted in a penitential direction. Consequently, the service detracted from, and obscured the celebratory character of the Eucharist as thanksgiving. In Sweden in the seventeenth and eighteenth centuries, Communion became a formal as well as a solemn requirement, and in 1686 a church law was promulgated requiring every citizen to communicate at least once a year. Thus Communion became a statuary civic requirement, and increasingly throughout the eighteenth century the majority of the population became infrequent communicants. This tendency towards infrequent Communion increased in the late eighteenth and the nineteenth centuries through the influence of the Pietists, who with their preoccupation with individual guilt, maintained that only the 'worthy guest' could approach the 'pure table of the Lord'. Ironically, the end result was that the formal legalism of the National Church, and the scrupulosity of the Pietists conspired to fence the altar, and effectively discourage people from making their Communion.

In the 1920s and 1930s, the main Sunday service in the majority of parishes in Sweden was the Högmässa, the High Mass, but this was in effect an antecommunion, a service which centred upon the sermon, the preaching of the Word. At these services the active involvement of the congregation was limited to the singing of hymns; the kind of hymns described by Gabriel in his Logbook as being subjective and obsessed with 'me' and 'my sin'. The Church in Sweden needed to be reminded of the sacramental, the objective and participatory dimensions of Christian worship. Gabriel's first visit to Sweden coincided with a period of liturgical renewal, and the recovery of the centrality of Communion in the worshipping life of the Church. A move which was envisioned by Söderblom, undergirded by the work of his son-in-law, Yngve Brilioth, and promoted by Gustav Aulén.

So, to conclude this section let us sketch-in some details concerning the Communion rite of the Swedish mass. Laurentius Petri had declared, like Cranmer in England, that the Communion was to be celebrated only when there were some to communicate with the priest, and this caveat became a basic principle in Swedish eucharistic theology and practice. Underlying this principle was the view, deeply rooted in Luther's teaching, that the act of Communion was the culmination and climax of the mass. Luther had taught that the act of Communion was the supreme means whereby the Christian participated most intimately in the fellowship of the whole Church. The sacred gifts received in Communion were to be received as a pledge of Christ's promise of eternal life. Such a view, made explicit in Luther's two catechisms, reinforced the notion of Communion as a gift, particularly the divine gift of the forgiveness of sins, of life and salvation. The gift was seen as being appropriated by faith, but was

objectively given. This aspect of Communion as gift is liturgically
expressed in the administration of Communion. As with all gifts, the
gift of Communion was something to be received. With this background understanding, we can now appreciate the reason why the
two priests presiding at the mass described by Gabriel, gave and
received the sacrament from each other, and so carefully and unhur-
riedly administered the sacrament to the kneeling communicants.
Gabriel's Swedish experience reminds us that Communion is pre-
eminently a gift, something which we receive from another, and as
one contemporary liturgical theologian, Robert Taft has recently
written, '. . . the Eucharist ideally at least, is not something one
takes. It is a gift received, a meal shared. And since sacraments by
their very nature are supposed to symbolise what they mean, then
self-service, cafeteria-style communion rites just will not do'.[4]

Daily Prayer

Gabriel's Logbook tells us that the young members of the Theologisk
Oratorium, in Denmark, were in the process of compiling a daily
office book for their own use as a praying community. They were
assisted in this task by the recently published Swedish Vesperale and
Psalterium, which they used as a model. The Swedish book provided
a form of morning and evening prayer, and compline, with the
appropriate psalmody set to simple plainsong tones. The material for
these three daily offices was drawn largely from the traditional
monastic offices of the Breviary. Historically the Breviary had been
abandoned in Sweden at the Reformation, and the modern Office
Book referred to here had a rather ambivalent status within the
Church of Sweden. It was not included within the official Church
Handbook, but curiously had received official authorisation for use
in the Church in 1915. Gabriel, it seems, was impressed with the
Office Book, and noted with some regret that 'it is entirely new as
yet to the congregations'. However, to complete the picture it should
be remembered that there are other traditions of daily prayer apart
from the Breviary tradition. Up until the Second World War, for
instance, there was in Sweden the common practice of family prayers,
and there was no lack of resources for this form of daily prayer.

In the 1920s and 1930s a number of initiatives were taken to
introduce the Daily Office to the Church of Sweden. This was largely
the work of the so-called High Church party, which in the 1930s was
led by a rather eccentric clergyman, Dr Gunnar Rosendal, who was

the vicar of Osby, a country parish midway between Lund and Växjö. Rosendal, it seems, had had some success in encouraging his parishioners to join him for the celebration of the daily office in his church. In a letter to Fr Tribe, dated 12 August 1936, Gabriel tells how on 'Friday we came to Rosendal's place – Osby. After dinner we went across to church, where fifty people were present at Compline, and sung it to plainsong ... Saturday, "Lauds" was at 9am, with twenty people present'. Rosendal's apparent success in promoting the celebration of the daily office in his parish had, it seems, some influence upon the clergy of Lund Cathedral, because having heard of developments at Osby, they instigated a weekly sung compline on Saturday nights at the Cathedral. Before long, this service was attracting a regular congregation of some seventy people.[5]

There were other initiatives in this area which were known and supported by Gabriel. There was a young parish priest Adell, in Lund, who edited a quarterly review of church music and liturgy, and who had been involved, together with Knut Peters, in the production of an office book, the Svensk tidegärd, which contained forms for Mattins, Lauds, Sext, Vespers and Compline, arranged for each day of the week and set to plainsong. Similar initiatives have been taken in more recent times, and a good example is the breviary style office book which was compiled by Lars Lindhagen, in 1969.

Church Renewal

In 1935, Rosendal set out his programme for renewal in a book, which took its title from the name of the high church movement, Kyrklig, förnyelse, or Church Renewal. The book appealed to the writings of Laurentius Petri, and dealt with questions concerning the sacraments of Baptism and Eucharist, holy Orders, and liturgical renewal. Rosendal had clearly trusted Gabriel's opinion and had used him as a confidant, and although Gabriel was not always in total sympathy with the aims and style of the movement, he was active in commending the movement to some of the bishops of the Swedish Church. Gabriel undoubtedly had some considerable influence upon Rosendal, and he was invariably candid in response to Rosendal's proposals. In one rather prolix letter to Rosendal, Gabriel attempts to focus what he considered ought to be the major aims of Church Renewal. Here, he writes. 'It seems to me that the essential points of Kyrklig förnyelse are these two: (1) Holy Communion as frequently as possible at the Högmässa, if possible every Sunday; (2)

daily liturgical prayers in the church. And it seems to me that Kyrklig förnyelse must base itself on the foundations laid by Luther, just as we Anglicans must go back to our seventeenth-century Fathers – not in order that we may stop there and treat them as infallible, but because they appealed in their turn to the Bible and the early church, and it is through them that the catholic Christian faith has come to us'.

Thus Gabriel encouraged Rosendal and his associates to dig deep into their own ecclesial traditions, for he was well aware that any renewal, any attempt to revitalise the Church's life, required a deliberate return to the sources of her own life. The purpose of such a return was not to discover some imagined golden age, but to untap, as it were, the original impulse of the Church's life, and to allow that impulse to carry the Church forward to meet the challenges and opportunities of the present time. Gabriel believed that the immediate task facing the Church Renewal movement was to convince the wider Church that the movement was credible and loyal to the history and ethos of the Church of Sweden. This task was clearly seen to be urgent, for Gabriel was anxious on account of the fact that some high church clergy might view Church Renewal as a possible platform from which to promote their more limited and ephemeral concerns. In a letter to Fr Tribe, dated 22 August 1936, Gabriel laments over the attitude of some high church clergy in Sweden who seemed to be too absorbed 'with externals and who singularly failed to make any real connections between theology, worship, and Christian life'. The eventual inclusion of such men in the ranks of Church Renewal led Gabriel to warn Rosendal of possible dangers. In the first place, he advised, the Church Renewal movement had to be careful not to give the impression that it was a ritualistic movement. Secondly, for the sake of their own integrity, and also to avoid the possibility of justifiable criticism from those sections of the Swedish Church whose sympathies they needed to win, the Church Renewal movement had to be prepared to accept the critical study of the Bible. Finally, Gabriel pleaded for a little more caution and a greater care in the way in which some vocal members of the movement were speaking of ministerial orders in the Church.

Recovering the Tradition

As we have seen, Gabriel urged Rosendal and those who supported the Church Renewal movement to engage with their own ecclesial traditions. In particular, he encouraged them to take a fresh and serious look at the teaching of Martin Luther. 'You are all', he claimed in a letter to Rosendal, 'Luther's children, and you must acknowledge your own father, and prove to everyone that the Kyrklig fornyelse is the expression in liturgy of Luther's own true meaning'. In his own mind, Gabriel was convinced that Luther's teaching, as distinct from that of Melancthon and later Lutheran orthodoxy, was consonant with an authentically catholic understanding of God and the economy of salvation. Admittedly Gabriel held certain reservations concerning Luther's revisions of the Mass, particularly the so-called German Mass, which he considered to be a deficient and defective liturgical form. If anything, such reservations added strength to the case of the Church Renewal movement to press for more adequate liturgical forms which would more fully express the rich nuances of Luther's teaching on the Eucharist.

In catholic circles in the Church of England, there was a general feeling of antipathy towards Luther. John Henry Newman, a father of the nineteenth century Oxford Movement, had denigrated Luther in the strongest possible terms in his discussion of the doctrine of Justification, and at one point, where he was considering the catholic orientation of via media, he declared that the spirit of Luther was dead. To some extent then, Newman must take some of the blame for the feeling of antipathy towards the German Reformer which was prevalent in the English Church, but on the whole, this feeling was born largely out of ignorance and prejudice. One exception, however, needs to be mentioned, and that is Fr Kelly of Kelham. In his Church History lectures on the Reformation, Kelly would speak of Luther as a prophet of the Church. Unsurprisingly, this view was adopted by his protegé, and in 1932, Gabriel was describing Luther as a prophet of the Christian Gospel, and as a protesting voice from *within* catholicism, declaring the message of apostolic Christianity, of God's action 'for us and for our salvation'.[6]

Having gained a positive estimate of Luther and his teaching, Gabriel was predisposed to read the work or Lutheran theologians, and as his proficiency in the Swedish language increased, so he began to read contemporary Swedish theological writing. Here he discovered a rich field of scholarship, and one which 'we in England needed to discover'. This strongly felt conviction led him to translate into English what he considered to be the best of contemporary Swedish theology, particularly the work of Brilioth, Gustav Aulén, and Anders Nygren. Gabriel produced the authorised English translation of Aulén's work on the doctrine of the Atonement in 1931, with the English title, *Christus Victor*. The book, which has achieved the status of a twentieth-century theological classic, was essentially a historical study, but one which went behind the dry scholastic and narrowly juridical doctrines of the Middle Ages and later era of Lutheran orthodoxy, and recovered the rich and varied imagery of the New Testament, which in turn had fired the theological thought of Patristic writers and Martin Luther. Aulén designated this converging thought and imagery, the 'classic view' of the atonement, a view which brought the suffering and death of Jesus into close proximity to the doctrine of the incarnation. The classic view of the atonement saw God himself entering into the human experience of life and death, through Jesus Christ, whose sacrifice on the cross of Calvary was the climax of a divine drama, a divine struggle and eventual triumph over the negative and destructive forces of sin and evil. In Gabriel's mind, such a view of the atonement succeeded in capturing and conveying the full force of the Christian Gospel. As he wrote in the translator's preface 'the-classic view of redemption is at once truly evangelical and truly catholic', and as such, was of the utmost ecumenical significance. 'Here, then, is the true hope of Reunion; not in the victory of 'Catholic' over 'Protestant', or of 'Protestant' over 'Catholic', but in the return of both to the rock whence they were hewn. There can be no true Reunion on the basis either of the Catholicism which delights to represent itself as the ideal religious system, or of the old Protestantism with its rigidity and its negations, or of the newer humanising, modernist Protestantism. Reunion is to come by the rediscovery of . . . the gospel of God's redemption, and to the richness of a Catholicism which is truly evangelical'.[7]

Gabriel held Professor Aulén in the greatest esteem and maintained a warm and personal relationship with him until the end of his life, and in an essay published by Bishop Leslie Hunter *The Scandinavian Churches*, (Faber, 1965), Gabriel reviewed his interest in Swedish theology, and included the following personal reminiscence of his last meeting with Gustav Aulén: 'In June 1961 I had the wonderful experience of dining with him again at Lund, in the house where he now lives. He is 84 now, but is still vigorous in mind; and his life has covered an eventful period. He always impressed one above all else as a great Christian. He is a musician, expert in church music and a hymn writer, a dogmatic theologian, a theologian of the eucharistic liturgy, and an ecumenist; for it is always with the catholic, or universal Christian faith that he is concerned, and not with the tenets

Canon Narborough, Bristol   Count Wachtmeiston   E. G. Gulin, Abo
Dr Brodersen, Copenhagen   Prof. Ording, Oslo   J. S. Boys-Smith, Cambridge
Prof. Nygren, Lund   Countess Wachtmeiston   A. C. Bouquet, Cambridge
Prof. Norregaard, Copenhagen   Prof. Brilioth, Lund   A. G. Hebert, Kelham
Prof. Aulén, Lund   Bishop of Middleton   Kammarkem Dickson   Master of Selwyn
Canon Quick, London   Prof. Runestam, Uppsala

Theological Conference Sparreholm, Sweden, 1–8 July 1931

Reading of the Gospel:
High Mass in the
Great Chapel, Kelham.
(1935)

The Thanksgiving Prayer:
High Mass in the
Great Chapel, Kelham.
(1935)

of some school of thought or party'. (*The Scandinavian Churches*, p. 128)

A Source of Liturgical Renewal

Gabriel's recognition of the significance of the work of theologians like Aulen, was a considerable achievement, and his translations of Swedish theology was undoubtedly a major contribution to the English-speaking theological world, but the work which most directly influenced his own thinking and writing was a study of the Eucharist by Yngve Brilioth.

Yngve Brilioth was an exceptionally gifted historian and linguist. Temperamentally he was shy, and like most people who are naturally cautious and withdrawn, he preferred to be invisible, but this did not prevent him from coming to the attention of Nathan Söderblom, who in 1915 enlisted him to be his personal secretary. Söderblom encouraged the young Brilioth in his interest in nineteenth-century English Church history, and in 1919, having married Söderblom's eldest daughter, Brita, came over to England to study the Oxford Movement. This research led to the publication, in 1925, of his book *The Anglican Revival*. The following year, having secured the chair of Ecclesiastical History, in the theology faculty of Åobo University, in Finland, Brilioth began to write what was to be a substantial study of the Eucharist. It was published in 1926, with the Swedish title, *Nattvarden i evangeliskt gudstjänstliv*. On his first visit to Sweden, Gabriel had taken with him a short note on the book, which had appeared in a recent edition of the journal *Theology*. Once he was able to read the book himself, Gabriel realised that Brilioth's work could be a powerful force for liturgical renewal, and a means of raising the sacramental consciousness of Christians, not only in Sweden, but also in England. In the spring of 1929, Gabriel published a review of the book in the Easter edition of the SSM Quarterly. Within twelve months Gabriel had submitted an English translation to Brilioth for correction. Brilioth had welcomed Gabriel's initiative, and had prepared a shorter text of his book for the proposed English translation. This translation appeared later in the year, with the English title. *Eucharistic Faith and Practice: Catholic and Evangelical.*

In writing the book, Brilioth had sought to counter some of the nineteenth-century theories concerning the origins and meaning of the Eucharist, and although the study precluded a discussion of the

Roman and Eastern eucharistic rites, it did provide a historical survey of the Reformers' teaching on the Eucharist. Extensive coverage was given on the work of Luther, Calvin and Zwingli, as well as an ecumenically sensitive discussion of the Anglican, Reformed, Scottish, and Swedish eucharistic rites. From such an historical analysis, the book proceeded to construct a comprehensive eucharistic theology, by arranging and interpreting the various liturgical and doctrinal material through a grid of five eucharistic motifs: (1) the Eucharist as thanksgiving; (2) Communion and fellowship; (3) commemoration, or the historical aspect; (4) the eucharistic sacrifice, and finally; (5) the mystery of the presence. The work had a considerable influence upon Gabriel's greatest work, and it comes as no surprise to discover that Brilioth's eucharistic study is the single most quoted book in his own *Liturgy and Society*. Today, *Eucharistic Faith and Practice* has long since been out of print. Its treatment of the New Testament and the Patristic period has been superceded by more recent scholarship, but as a source for the study of Lutheran liturgy, it continues to be an important text, and for the student of the history of Anglican eucharistic theory and practice, it can also repay serious attention. Its conclusion, however, seems to capture an insight of abiding significance, and provides an apt conclusion to this account of Gabriel Hebert's Scandinavian connection. 'We have tried to show that in the Eucharist there are both a manifoldness of diverse aspects and a central unity; just as the jewel shows endless changes of light and colour as it is regarded from different angles. But the light which it refracts is one and the same: the holy Presence, the Mystery. It is true to say that the other aspects of the Eucharist are only different sides of the Mystery, or, from the human point of view, different ways of approaching it; and the various forms of liturgy and systems of doctrine which we have surveyed have helped to show the richness of its variety in constantly changing forms. But it is also true that since the early centuries no part of Christendom has succeeded in expressing all the aspects together, in their harmony and completeness. Is it over-bold to look forward in hope to a future day when a fuller unity of Christendom shall again reveal the great Christian sacrament in the wholeness of its many-sided glory'.
(*Eucharistic Faith and Practice*, p. 288)

3
ECUMENISM AND WORSHIP

In the 1920s, as in the years immediately prior to the Great War, Fr Kelly, together with SSM brethren and students, became a familiar sight at the Student Christian Movement conferences which were held at Swanwick in Derbyshire. In many ways, the story of the SCM and the SSM are closely tied together, and Fr Kelly emerges as the quirky character who rarely appeared centre stage, and yet, managed to exert a wise and challenging influence upon the outlook and ethos of both organisations.

The origins of the SCM can be traced back to the Inter University Christian Union, which flourished in Britain in the 1890s, and formed a sizable network of young and able evangelical Christians. Between 1907 and 1909, a number of individuals within this loose affiliation of young Christians began to seek ways of relating what they considered to be the fundamentals of Christian faith to the challenges and insights of contemporary thought. From these stirrings emerged the fledgling SCM. A decisive break was made from the annual evangelical Convention at Keswick, and various college and university groups began to realign themselves and adopt either a Christian Union, or an SCM outlook. Both bodies continued to be inter-denominational, but the SCM was anxious to widen its clientèle and actively sought the participation of those with a more catholic perspective. Even so, there were some who were uneasy about the SCM appearing to be influenced by those whom they considered to be too High Church. Tissington Tatlow in his lengthy book *The Story of the Student Christian Movement*, (SCM 1933), admits that 'Fr Kelly's cassock at the Summer Conferences, and the appearance of men like Canon Scott Holland and Bishop Gore on the platform caused me no little trouble behind the scenes'. (p. 386)

The shift in attitude amongst student Christians was not an easy passage, and some groups wavered in their allegiance. The Christian Union at Cambridge, for instance, became suspicious of the SCM approach, and in March 1910 decided to preserve their evangelical pedigree by becoming an independent body (CICCU) without any formal affiliation with the SCM.

After his return from South Africa, Gabriel often accompanied Fr Kelly to the SCM Conferences, and probably more than anyone else, helped people to see the point which the 'old man' was driving at. In this way, Gabriel was not only Kelly's protégé, but also his interpreter to an all too often bemused audience. He was present on the celebrated occasion when Fr Kelly addressed the Swanwick Conference in July 1927, and began with these rather puzzling words. 'We are met in the most holy name of religion. I am not quite sure what people mean by that most heathen word, (never used of Christianity in the New Testament), but my business is to talk about God, which is not quite the same thing'.

True to character, Kelly was calling his audience back to consider basic principles. His expressed intention was to talk about God, and to talk about God not in some glib and easy way, or in a way which might signal some ecclesiastical party loyalty, but to enunciate the Gospel. Indeed, what is arguably Kelly's greatest book, *The Gospel of God*, is an enlarged and much expanded version of this particular address. The greatness of the book consists in the fact that it is the best record of both the style and content of Fr Kelly's teaching. In his review of the book, Gabriel argues that although the book was clumsily written, and in parts awkwardly expressed, it nevertheless succeeded in delivering the full prophetic force of Fr Kelly's teaching.[1]

The understanding of the Christian faith offered by Kelly in *The Gospel of God*, recalls the teaching of F.D.Maurice, and in turn, the view of the poet and philosopher, Samuel Taylor Coleridge, for whom Christianity was neither a theory, nor a speculation, but 'a life and a living process'. So, in a somewhat similar vein, Kelly speaks of the Christian faith not as some interior and spiritual endeavour, or in terms of a coherent system of beliefs, but in existential and personal terms. In Kelly's view, Christian faith was primarily a personal letting-go, and a voluntary submission of the self to the influence of the God who acts, and who acts purposefully. For Kelly this action, and this purpose, was seen to be primarily focused and demonstrated in the incarnate life, death and resurrection of Jesus Christ. Here, and here alone, was seen the divine answer to the human quandary and search for meaning and purpose, and here, and here supremely, was demonstrated the divine solidarity with human suffering and tragedy.

Such a radical presentation of the Christian story and its adventure of faith, was made by a man who was both an independent thinker and a loyal and fully committed churchman, and this aspect of his personality probably had some impact and influence upon the thinking and outlook of the SCM, particularly as it came to articulate its inter-denominational, as opposed to a non-denominational, policy. As a loyal churchman, Kelly was convinced that any genuine attempt to live the Christian life had to be firmly rooted in the life and worship of a local Christian community, a local church. This view led him to argue that the various denominations mattered, and to encourage the members of the SCM to be loyal to the churches which had awakened and nurtured their faith. For only in this way, he paradoxically believed, could individuals come to recognise the full scandal of Christian disunity.

Denomintions and the Church

Kelly had long argued that the reality of a divided Church was a fact which had to be honestly faced and fully recognised, and he frequently insisted that the first step along the ecumenical path was such a recognition. What he wanted people to realise was that the differences between the denominations were significant, as each possibly represented an aspect of Christian truth, and so these differences were not to be ignored, or lightly dismissed as a result of historic accident, or of simply a past of an earlier generation's making, but were to be admitted, acknowledged and understood. As he said, it is precisely these differences which are the difficulties and challenge of ecumenism.

It seems as though Fr Kelly never deviated from this outlook and approach to the task of ecumenism, an approach which was clearly and concisely expressed in a pamphlet which he wrote in 1915, and which set out what he considered to be the realistic expectations of an ecumenical gathering: 'The purpose of the Conference is a better understanding of the convictions of other people . . . The method of the Conference is enquiry. Our search should be directed not so much to the discovery of agreements, as to an appreciation of differences.

. . . New agreements may arise if it develops that common convictions are embodied in divergent expressions; but we must not be disappointed if we are unable to perceive changes of really opposing convictions. On the contrary, we should be well satisfied if all parties, or even some parties, come to understand better than before what their essential differences are, and what new aspects of truth they represented'.[2]

The kind of approach to ecumenical discussions expressed by Fr Kelly was undoubtedly adopted by Gabriel in his own ecumenical discussions and involvements, and this is clearly seen in his involvement with the SCM. He was not only a frequent participant in the SCM camps at Swanwick, but also had a hand in the actual planning and policy making of the Movement as a member of the Council.

In an undated letter to Fr Reginald Tribe, Gabriel describes how some of the travelling secretaries of the SCM were grappling with what he described as the problem of denominationalism, and seeking for an understanding of the Church in which the various denominations might be seen to make their own positive contribution. In a phrase which is reminiscent of the thought of F.D.Maurice, Gabriel ventures to say that what they require is 'a vision of the Church as the Kingdom of Christ within whose unity the denominations have their contribution to bring'.[3]

As we shall see, Gabriel was under no illusion regarding the sheer complexity of the questions surrounding the issue of Christian unity and Communion between the Churches. In many ways, the SCM provided an important forum for the discussion of these questions, but developments overseas were making the issue more urgent and immediate. The most significant development overseas was the proposed scheme of Union for the Church of South India. This scheme, officially proposed in 1929, sought to bring into a single body the Anglican, Presbyterian, Congregational, Lutheran and Methodist churches in South India.

In a missionary situation, the issues which had historically divided the Church seemed remote, if not irrelevent, and this feeling had been growing for well over the past twenty years. Indeed, the now famous World Missionary Societies Conference which met at Edinburgh in 1910, commonly regarded as marking the real beginning of the twentieth-century Ecumenical Movement, provided an occasion when individuals working in the mission field could ventilate some of the frustration they felt at the unnecessary competition and duplication which inevitably arose in areas where more than one denomination was at work.

The conference was a predominantly Evangelical and Free Church gathering. The Anglo-Catholic missionary society, the SPG, had been invited, but had declined the invitation. However, there were delegates of a more catholic outlook, including Neville Talbot, Charles Gore and Fr Kelly, and from his autobiographical jottings, it is clear that Kelly regarded the Edinburgh conference as being a momentous and opportune occasion. Through its deliberations the conference had recognised the imperative of Christian unity, and acknowledged the unhappy fact that the disunity of the churches blunted the impact of Christian outreach to non-Christian cultures, and seriously jeopardised the effectiveness of missionary initiatives, not only in evangelism, but also in the provision of health care and educational opportunity. Such pragmatic considerations gave the question of Christian unity a greater urgency, but for some, there was also a theological imperative, the need for the churches to speak of, and visibly show, the unity which the whole of humanity has in Christ Jesus, the second Adam. This universal and theological challenge was regarded by some as being the particular challenge which God was presenting to the Church in the twentieth century. The difficulty of this challenge was that a divided Church could hardly witness to the unity of all people in Christ. Hence, ecumenism, a process of reconciling the different churches and promoting a more co-operative witness, was seen as the first major step in meeting this challenge.

The question of how exactly the churches might be reconciled and on what basis, has dogged the Christian churches throughout this ecumenical century. For some, the immediate strategy has been to seek ways of reconciling the structures and ministries of the different churches, and for others, the ecumenical challenge has demanded the removal of inessentials, those matters indifferent, and a coming together of the various Christian bodies around a recognised and agreed kernel of Christian revelation. This second strategy might well appear to be the most radical procedure, but it is not without its own dangers. There is the risk, for instance, of regarding as inessential something which might well be given by God. Fr Kelly would certainly have repudiated what today might be seen as being a reductionist approach to the challenge of Christian unity. He certainly was unconvinced by those who were seeking 'the essence of the Christian proclamation' in order to provide a basis and sine qua non of Christian unity, and himself maintained that ecumenical discussion should lead to an enlargement of the Christian's understanding and experience of the Church, her ministry and sacramental worship – and this was the lesson he had learnt at Edinburgh 1910. As he wrote in his autobiographical jottings. 'There were many who were naturally inclined to minimise differences, to fall back upon the comfortable "we are all going the same way" style of talking, especially in the early stages. However, as discussions became deeper, so people became more conscious of the particularity and value of their respective ecclesial traditions. . . . But as we got to know other people better . . . we all began to realise better our own position, and the value of what God had given them'.[4]

The lesson Kelly had learnt at the Edinburgh conference was that real ecumenism sprang from a theological imperative as well as from more pragmatic considerations concerning the Church's mission. Furthermore, the ecumenical process itself could not adequately proceed from the basis of the lowest common denominator. Like the early twentieth-century French Modernists, he realised that those things which many might consider to be mere inessentials, or external to the supposed heart of Christian faith and life, might be of the utmost significance in maintaining a sense of Christian identity.

The ecumenical process envisaged in the Proposed Scheme for the inauguration of a united Church of South India rested upon a very different basis. The first objective in this proposed scheme was to foster a spirit of unity among the churches, and not to set in place, as is sometimes assumed today, a new structure of Church order and government. The proposals certainly did speak of an eventual recon-ciliation of ministries within the churches, and of intercommunion between the covenanting churches; but these things were expressed in terms of aims rather than immediate objectives. In speaking of intercommunion, the proposals stated that such a practice was to be seen as the fruit of the spirit of unity, and not as a means of achieving that aim. For intercommunion to signify all that it should signify, there first had to be a real growing together in the faith and order of the Church. Implicit in this view is the conviction that Christians must first appreciate the implications of their Baptism, of what it means to be in Christ, if they are to avoid the stricture of St Paul. 'It is not the Lord's Supper which you eat'. In other words, intercommunion between the separated churches was not to be regarded as a means to an end, but the result of a real growing together in unity and truth. Such an outlook harboured a certain ecumenical reserve, a keeping back of eucharistic hospitality until that time when there was a palpable fellowship and conscious participation in the fulness of the Church's faith and ordered life.

Regarding this ordering of the Church, the proposals spoke of an eventual coming together of episcopally ordained and non-episcopally ordained ministers, and expressed a hope of a joint growing together within the historic threefold ministry of bishops, priests and deacons. The declared expectation was that 'eventually every minister exercising a permanent ministry in the united church will be an episcopally ordained minister'.[5] For Presbyterians and Congregationalists such an aim was a gigantic shift of outlook and policy. Nevertheless, in South India they were clearly persuaded by the force of Christian history and tradition, and agreed to accept episcopacy as the primary means of holding together and regulating the life of the envisaged United Church. However, it should be noted that what the participating churches in this scheme were actually agreeing to and opting for, was 'constitutional episcopacy', which, as such, did not imply or entail the endorsement of any one theory, or theological understanding of the episcopal office, or of episcopal ordination. For Anglo-Catholic critics of this scheme, this was the fatal flaw, and their persistent complaint was that the proposed scheme could only result in a compromise of 'catholic order.' This allegation fuelled a controversy which raged in England until the outbreak of the Second World War, and was ventilated, sometimes in the most virulent terms, in the correspondence columns and editorials of the *Church Times*. Amongst the published letters of protest against the Scheme, was one signed by the Superiors of the major Anglican Religious Communities, but significantly, the name of the Director of the Society of the Sacred Mission was not included.

'We are all in schism, and we all fall short of the fulness of catholicity'

In his *Intercommunion: A theological study of Christian Unity*, (SPCK 1932), Gabriel welcomes the South India Scheme for reunion and speaks of it in the most effusive terms as a cause for thanksgiving and hope for the future. The proposals, he claimed, were realistic and practicable, and he commended the scheme especially for the way in which it envisioned a structural reunion of the churches, not as the the consummation of Christian unity, but as a setting in place and creation of those conditions in which Christians from the various denominations might grow together in unity and come to the fulness of Christian *koinonia*. Such a positive estimate of the South India Scheme was part of a whole book which was intentionally and intrinsically eirenic in tone and lucidly written.

In this book Gabriel expresses his gratitude to the many Free Church friends and contacts he had made through the SCM, and sets himself the task of explaining to these friends, in as generous and honest a way as he was able, something of his own perception of the problems facing the task of Christian reunion, and of giving a reasoned account of his own loyalties and convictions concerning the nature of the Church, her sacramental ministry, and the way towards reunion. Unsurprisingly, he takes the thought of F.D.Maurice as the framework for his own arguments, and sets out to explain the view that the Church was both a human and a divine institution, given, as it were, to make tangible in the world, the catholicity of God's dealings with humanity. In Maurician terms, the Church was a God-given sign of the universal Kingdom of Christ, and the threefold ministry of bishops, priest and deacons, Gabriel argues, was providentially given to the Church to secure her continuity and continuance as a focus and instrument of God's Kingdom and Covenant in every age and place. Although Gabriel's views are considered and carefully argued, he writes with obvious conviction, and in certain points in the book, his judgements are forcefully stated. This is especially the case where he deals with the sensitive question as to how the desired reunion of the churches might properly proceed. He is quick, for instance, to repudiate any procedure which might imply, on the part of any one church, an element of spiritual imperialism, such as might occur if the Church of England were to yield to the Roman claim of Papal infallibility. Gabriel is equally strident in dismissing any doctrinaire approach which might take a point of ecclesiology, such as the doctrine of apostolic succession, and use it as a means of effectively unchurching another denomination. To use the doctrine of apostolic succession in this way, according to Gabriel, was more indicative of a sectarian attitude than of a real and living sense of the catholicity of the Church.

The full thrust of Gabriel's argument in this book is that the principles underlying our understanding of the nature of the Church and her ministry, ought to be the real substance of ecumenical dialogue and discussion, and he is unequivocal in his opinion that these same principles should not be misused by simply point scoring, or attempting to claim the high ground in a discussion. Even, he says, in the event of a non-episcopal church accepting the principle of episcopal ordination, there should not be any talk which might suggest 'the victory of one denomination over the rest'.[6] The truly important purpose and aim of ecumenical discussion can only be the growth of all Christians into a more perfect catholicity.

Another book, much shorter and certainly more rhetorical in style, was published by Gabriel some seven years after his volume *Intercommunion*. This shorter book, entitled *Unity in the Truth* (SPCK 1939), provides the reader with quite a marked contrast. For this book, little more than an outgrown pamphlet, was a response, written in an unfortunate combative style, to the outline of a scheme for the reunion of the Evangelical Free Churches of England and the Church of England. The outline in question had been drawn up by a joint conference of Anglicans and Free Churchmen, which had been officially appointed for the purpose by the Archbishop of Canterbury, Cosmo Gordon Lang, and the Federal Free Church Council. What the outline proposed was to a large extent inspired by the principles which had shaped the scheme for the reunion of the churches in South India. Superficially, it seems odd that Gabriel could vehemently argue against the scheme for an English reunion of churches, and yet welcome what might reasonably be called its parent scheme, the scheme which eventually brought into being in 1947, the Church of South India. The reader might well be excused for detecting an inconsistency in Gabriel's professed position vis à vis these two schemes. However, a closer reading of this more polemical work does show that Gabriel's reservations concerning the proposed English church reunion scheme were not entirely unjustifiable. The proper desire for the reunion of the English churches was being carried forward by a wave of new found national unity, as Britain found herself on the verge of war with Germany, and it was not unreasonable to sound a note of caution. However desirable the end, no single scheme for the reunion of the churches should be carried forward solely by the force of jingoist sentiment. In this light, Gabriel is not seen as being obstructive, but as sounding a note of caution and calling again for a more conscious and deliberate consideration of the theological principles at stake in the whole debate on Christian unity. In this, he was acting in accordance with the aims of his mentor, Fr Herbert Kelly, who was constant in his demands for theological rigour.

Regarding the proposed outline for the reunion between Free Churchmen and Christians in the established and national Church, Gabriel was also anxious that the Roman Church and the Orthodox Churches should not be excluded from the ecumenical horizon. Thus in *Unity in the Truth*, Gabriel insists that these two major Christian families should be kept in view in any proposed scheme for the reunion of estranged churches. In this, Gabriel was ably supported by George Every, a brilliant lay theologian at Kelham and SSM brother, who wrote a tightly argued appendix to *Unity in the Truth*, highlighting the wider ecumenical implications of the English reunion scheme. Undoubtedly, there were other factors and influences which led Gabriel to write *Unity in the Truth*, and which resulted in its rather negative tone. Indeed, as we shall shortly see, there were reasons which led Gabriel to part company with some Anglican and Free Church friends in the late 1930s. An impatience to see some structural and institutional reunion of the churches, it seems, has never really helped the protracted, and sometimes painful, way of ecumenism.

Open Communion

At large ecumenical gatherings, like the SCM conferences, Gabriel had long warned against using the practice of 'open communion' as a palliative for the pain caused by the disunity of the churches. The Lambeth Conference of 1930 had discussed the matter, and resolved that intercommunion 'should be the goal of, rather than a means to, the restoration of union', (resolution 40). This was the definitive ruling, but a vaguer statement was added to the effect that baptised communicants of another denomination might receive Communion in an Anglican church 'when the ministrations of their own church are not available, or in special, or temporary circumstances'. The problem, of course, was knowing to what circumstances these conditions might pertain. Requests for joint Communion services were being made at large ecumenical gatherings, such as the SCM camps and conferences, and Gabriel realised that the spirit of unity fostered on these occasions required some formal and corporate expression, and in an article entitled 'Open Communion', he suggested the adoption of the Agape, the convivial fellowship meal which was practised in the early Church, and was restored with some success in the early days of Methodism.[7] Here indeed was a practicable solution, which Gabriel believed would be widely accepted. In this article, Gabriel also encouraged Anglicans and Non-Conformists to attend each others' services in order to grow in mutual understanding, but he was adamant in his insistence that they should not go so far as receiving the sacrament from each others' altars. In his view, to take that step of intercommunion, at that time, would be to preempt the necessarily long process of ecumenical dialogue which lay ahead. A proper dialogue, a real meeting of minds and ecclesial traditions of worship and ministry, was, in Gabiel's mind, the prerequisite and condition of ecumenical progress. Furthermore, such ecumenical dialogue had to engage with a theological agenda, and go beyond the level of political strategies and institutional structures. As he said '... at interdenominational meetings for the study of reunion it is a waste of time to discuss plans for reunion ... We ought rather to study the fundamental principles of theology, the meaning of salvation, and grace and baptism'.[8]

Gabriel was particularly unhappy about the possibility of those situations arising, where an open Communion might be used as a means of expressing a group's sense of solidarity and fellow-feeling. To do this, he thought, would be a misuse of the sacrament. The Eucharist was not primarily a means for expressing human feelings, or aspirations, but rather, a vehicle for expressing that for which it had been divinely appointed and instituted, namely, the objective commemoration of God's saving work in Christ. In these terms, Gabriel countered the demands of the ecumenical enthusiasts, and made the point that the goal of reunion was the reconciliation of the divided churches, and not the setting up of arbitrary groups of like-minded people. So, in a rather polemical passage in *Open Communion* he roundly concludes, 'I want reunion with the traditions, with these churches, not with scattered individuals torn away from the roots out of which they have grown'.[9]

The line of argument and the tone of this article resulted, at least in part, from Gabriel's experience of an organisation called the Friends of Reunion. This organisation came into being at a conference which was held at High Leigh, on 15 and 16 May 1933. The inspiration behind this conference, which brought together members of the Anglican and British Free Churches, had been generated by the World Faith and Order Conference held at Lausanne in August 1927. That conference, a major event in the history of ecumenism, had brought together a large and international gathering of Christians, representing the Orthodox, Oriental, Anglican, Protestant churches, as well as delegates from the numerically smaller, but significant Old Catholic and Mennonite churches, and the Society of Friends.

The High Leigh conference was officially sponsored by the continuation committee of the Lausanne conference, which was ably chaired by the Archbishop of York, William Temple. At the Lausanne conference the Anglican church achieved a fairly high profile, and it was there that the idea that the Anglican church might act as an ecumenical bridge church, and provide a wide ecumenical meeting ground, gained currency. This view undoubtedly bolstered Anglican confidence that they were well placed to promote the ecumenical cause. At High Leigh there were many who were anxious to quicken the pace of reunion between the Church of England and the Free Churches, and in an optimistic mood, the conference resolved to promote 'in every village, town and city' ecumenical groups for prayer and study.

Gabriel was present at the High Leigh conference, but as we shall see, his commitment to the Friends of Reunion was not entirely single-hearted, and his impressions of the inaugural conference were hardly flattering or commendatory. He was profoundly unhappy about the conference worship, particularly those sessions led by Anglicans who aped the Free Church tradition of extempore prayer, and which came across as hollow and inauthentic. On the whole, he felt that the worship at High Leigh was drab and pedestrian. Regarding the conference itself, Gabriel detected an unwillingness on the part of the participants to grasp the theological nettle. There were, he thought, a whole cluster of theological issues which required attention, and the most pressing of these revolved around the question of belief, more specifically, the question of the relationship between beliefs and Christian identity. The first step, Gabriel felt, was that the conference should recognise the sheer diversity of beliefs which it represented, and then face the question as to whether such a variety of beliefs could be contained within a coherent pattern of Christian believing. As it was, the conference was inclined to duck the issue, and in Gabriel's reading of the situation, to simply ignore this question was, in effect, to opt for 'the conformity of opinion'. This option could hardly provide a sufficient and satisfactory basis upon which to construct a scheme for the reunion of the churches. Again, he insisted, differences of belief had to be faced, because beliefs mattered, and mattered more than opinions.

Underlying Gabriel's persistent concern with differences of belief, was not so much an adherence to a propositional view of Christian revelation, as the nagging and difficult question of what exactly a person had to believe in order to be properly identified as a Christian. In his own reflections on this matter, he wondered, as a possible example, whether the expressed beliefs of a Christian Scientist would be seen to fall within the parameters of orthodox Christian belief. For Gabriel, this was no mere academic exercise, but posed a real quandary. What was clear in his own mind, was that beliefs and personal identity were inextricably bound together, and that being a professed Christian entailed the holding of certain, and in principle, statable beliefs. It would be a gross misrepresentation of Gabriel's position in this matter to suggest that he wanted to exclude certain people from the Christian arena; on the contrary, what he sought was a greater clarity of thought and a willingness to face the questions. It would be equally a misrepresentation to suggest that for the Friends of Reunion the question of beliefs was a question of 'anything goes'; such an attitude could only spring from a total theological bankruptcy. The situation, as read by Gabriel, was that there was a tendency to fudge the important issues, and for Gabriel, what he wanted was not a doctrinal exactitude, but to bring ecumenical discussion into dialogue with the most searching theological questions.

However, despite, or possibly because of these convictions, Gabriel was elected at the inaugural conference to serve on the Council of Friends of Reunion. In itself, this fact is ample evidence to show that he made a good impression on a good number of delegates. Nevertheless his attitude towards the organisation was ambivalent, and at that time, considering himself to be a card carrying Anglo-Catholic, he admitted that 'if we stay out, they'll go on without us'.[10]

The Ever Widening Circle

The decade between 1928 and 1938 was a decade of intense ecumenical activity, and during this period Gabriel was making an ever increasing circle of contacts with other churches. As the writer of his obituary in the Church Times put it, 'At times his brethren found it difficult to keep pace with him'.[11] From the point of view of Gabriel's contribution to British theology, the most significant of these contacts were, as we shall see, with the Lutheran churches in Sweden and Denmark, and with Roman Catholics on the continent, who were involved in the Liturgical Movement. John Perret's cartoon showing Gabriel heading off towards the ecumenical fog, clutching a bag on which is written, 'ecumenical plot', humorously captures the fact that Gabriel was a frequent attender at ecumenical meetings and conferences. In August 1932, for instance, Gabriel took part in an ecumenical retreat which was held at De Mouterhouse, which included such notable ecumenists and scholars as Dr Visser'tHooft, Nicholas Zernov, and Professor Gustav Aulen, all of whom we shall hear of shortly. Again, Bishop George Bell, the Bishop of Chichester, certainly regarded Gabriel as an important and useful link person as he set about planning his own ecumenical initiatives and projects.

Undoubtedly, Gabriel was reckoned as being a person who was well able to make contributions at ecumenical meetings, and these in turn must have influenced and enriched his own developing notion of the catholicity of the Church.

In England, as we have seen, the SCM provided Gabriel with a rich ecumenical meeting ground and forum for discussion and exchange, and there was also the Fellowship of Saint Alban and Saint Sergius, whose conferences brought together a constellation of Anglican, Orthodox and Free Church theologians, including Oliver Quick, V. A. Demant, Lionel Thornton C.R., and Nathanial Micklem, and attracted a number of intelligent and committed young Christians.

Throughout the 1930s gigantic strides were taken in bringing the Anglican and Orthodox churches into a closer relationship. The most celebrated occasion in this regard, was the meeting of Anglicans and Romanian Orthodox, at Bucharest in June 1935, when understanding between the two churches advanced at an astonishing rate. In fact, in the March of the following year, the Holy Synod of the Romanian Orthodox Church came within a whisker's breadth of recognising the validity of Anglican Orders, and resolved that exploratory meetings between the two churches should be 'continued in the future until the Holy Spirit pour out his grace to make clear that the doctrines of the Anglican Church are in complete agreement with the doctrine of the Orthodox Oecumenical Church'.

The following month, April 1936, an important meeting between Anglican and Orthodox theologians, (the Orthodox being part of the Russian emigré community in Paris), took place at the House of the Resurrection, at Mirfield. At this residential three day meeting, which took place from 28 to 30 April, there were frank exchanges between the delegates, and theological differences were honestly faced. But this serious discussion was conducted in the most convivial atmosphere, and was wisely presided over by Bishop Walter Frere C.R. Apart from some other C.R. brethren, the Anglican contingent included Dom Gregory Dix, Eric Mascall and Gabriel. On this occasion, Gabriel was able to contribute to the kind of theological dialogue, which, he believed, was demanded by the very seriousness of ecumenism, and to which he was wholeheartedly committed. The success and significance of this meeting is documented by Nicholas Zernov, in his book *The Russian Religious Renaissance of the Twentieth Century* (DLT, 1963), and there he laments the fact that with Bishop Frere's death in 1938, and the outbreak of the Second World War in 1939, the very promising ecumenical discussions between Anglicans and Orthodox were brought to an abrupt and premature halt.

As well as having the opportunity to meet and talk with Orthodox Christians, Gabriel also had a number of opportunities to meet and speak with Roman Catholics. At that time, however, Roman Catholics were not officially allowed to take part in ecumenical discussions and meetings. Nevertheless, meetings of a more informal nature did take place, and important friendships were made. Gabriel and other SSM brethren, for example, met on a regular basis for theological discussions with English Dominicans at the Blackfriars School at Laxton, in Stamford. Again, being based at Kelham, meant that Gabriel was able to meet and talk with people from the whole ecumenical spectrum, as there were many from different churches and communions who were attracted to the place. One of these visitors, the Abbé Paul Couturier, has been hailed as 'the apostle of unity', and so it is appropriate that something of his story be recorded here.

Since his ordination as a young priest, Fr Paul Couturier had made a practice of celebrating the holy mysteries on St Bartholomew's day, 24 August, as an act of penitence and sorrow for the pillage and massacre of the Huguenots on that day by Catholics in 1572. Furthermore, throughout his own quiet and faithful ministry at Lyons, Fr Couturier had encouraged many to pray, particularly throughout the week in which St Bartholomew's day occurred, for that unity which Christ willed for his people. In July 1938, during a trip to England, Fr Couturier paid a visit to Kelham and was invited to speak informally to a gathering of students and brethren in the Common Room. What he said on that occasion obviously struck a very deep note in the hearts of many in his audience. He certainly made a deep and lasting impression upon Gabriel, who some years later wrote a lucid and compelling article in which he outlined the the aims and singular importance of the Week of Prayer for Christian Unity. This week was to be a week of prayer and, as Gabriel stated the matter, the prayer offered to God at this time ought not be prayer *for* any particular scheme, or strategy for the reunion of the churches, but rather 'prayer directed towards the realising in all parts of divided Christendom of the true pattern of faith and worship and way of life'.[12] This phrase, so simply expressed, probably best encapsulates Gabriel's most mature ecumenical conviction, the conviction that the proper reunion of the churches will manifest, in all aspects of its life and witness, the full catholicity of the Church.

The full measure of Fr Couturier's influence upon Gabriel is most clearly seen in what was undoubtedly Gabriel's greatest ecumenical achievement, namely his considerable part in establishing the Week of Prayer for Christian Unity in Australia. The Week which fell in the week of 18 to 25 January, was something to which he was keenly committed to the end of his life. Gabriel returned to Kelham from St Michael's House, Adelaide, in 1961, and amongst his papers from this latter period is a memo, written in minuscule letters and with an unsteady hand, to the Prior of Kelham, Fr Theodore Smith, (who lacked both the charisma and the confidence of his predecessor, Fr Stephen Bedale), lamenting that the observance of the Week of Prayer in 1962 had seemed rather tired and tame, and so Gabriel was offering some practical suggestions as to how the observance of the Week might be arranged in subsequent years, so that their prayer for unity might feel a little more urgent and real.

The level of commitment to the cause of Christian Unity which Gabriel showed, especially in his years in Australia (1952–1961), was something which had been developing and deepening through many years of ecumenical discussion and debate. Unfortunately, some of this discussion had led to unresolved disagreements and dissention, and it is on this darker note that we must return to the final episode in Gabriel's involvement with the Friends of Reunion in the mid-1930s.

Intercommunion Revisited

Given the background, it is not surprising that Gabriel's most serious rift and eventual break with the Friends of Reunion organisation was precipitated by the issue of open Communion. The executive committee of the Friends of Reunion had proposed having an open celebration of Communion at the annual conference in 1934. Such a celebration, in the context of an ecumenical gathering, would have been legitimate under the current Anglican rulings, with the proviso that the proposed open Communion had received the consent of the appropriate Church of England diocesan bishop. In the event, such an episcopal consent was not granted. The situation was sadly and relunctuntly accepted by the Council of the Friends of Reunion, whose primary responsibility was the election of the executive committee. When the time came for planning the annual conference in 1935, feelings among members of the Council were running high, and there was certainly a general feeling of belligerence, with the majority of the Council members even more determined that there should be a celebration of an open Communion at the conference. When the Council met to discuss the matter, Gabriel clashed with the distinguished Congregationalist scholar C. H. Dodd who was wholeheartedly behind the proposal and totally convinced of its appropriateness. However, the disagreement between the two men was so serious and substantial, that Gabriel felt that his only option was to resign from the Council. The incident was reported by the Religious Affairs correspondent of the *Manchester Guardian* in these terms. 'Fr Hebert ssm, the Revd Hugh Martin and Professor Dodd ... spoke on the subject (Intercommunion) from different angles, and though there was some sharp division of opinion, every speech was worthy of its high subject and free from controversial spirit'.[13]

Gabriel considered this article to be a piece of anodyne reporting, and subsequently wrote to the editor in order to explain the gravity of the disagreement and its sorry consequence. Gabriel was anxious to provide the full picture of the situation, and carefully stated in his letter that what was a issue in the reported incident, was not a mere clash of opinion, but a serious conflict of principle, and that this had regrettably led him to render his resignation as a member of the Council. Even with hindsight, it is not easy to evaluate Gabriel's action over this matter. At one level his behaviour might seem to have been a little inconsistent, for having assisted to launch the boat, as it were, he then refused to ride the storm. On the other hand, it is transparent that Gabriel was faithful to his catholic principles, and that his convictions were deeply felt; but perhaps such a dogged adhesion to principles was indicative of a little intellectual pride.

From the outset, Hugh Martin, the Anglican priest who became the secretary of the Friends of Reunion, had not always followed or felt much sympathy with Gabriel's expressed views, and in the end, he was clearly exasperated by Gabriel's apparent *volte-face*. In a letter written to Gabriel on 14 January 1938, soon after Gabriel had made a complete break with the Friends of Reunion, Hugh Martin wrote, 'I think if you are going to wait for Rome you are delaying the whole thing until the Greek Kalends. In my judgement the Romans will be much more ready to talk seriously with a united "Protestantism"'.[14]

On this latter point the two men would never agree. Indeed, on the basis of his own contacts and exchanges, Gabriel was confident that Rome would soon officially enter the arena of ecumenical debate. In this, his hope was vindicated, albeit some ten years later, with the promulgation of Pope Pius XII's encyclical, 'De Motione Oecumenica', which was published by the Holy Office on 20 December 1949. Ecumenical progress, of course, had been halted by the hostilities of the Second World War, but in the late 1930s, Gabriel believed that an ecumenical breakthrough was about to occur. The basis for this confidence was the work of a French Dominican theologian, Fr M. J. Congar OP. In fact, there is a perfect irony that at the precise time when Hugh Martin was accusing Gabriel of being obstructive and of employing delaying tactics, an important article by Gabriel, entitled, 'Rome and Reunion', was published in the journal *Theology*. The substance of this article was an extended review of Congar's book, *Chrétiens désunis: principes d'un 'oecumen-isme' catholique* (Paris 1937), which Gabriel read as a positive sign that Roman Catholics were engaging with the ecumenical process. Gabriel regarded the book as a substantial contribution to the ecumenical debate, and saw in the general lines of its argument a possible ground-plan for a broadly based ecumenism. It offered a critical history of the causes of the Church's disunity, and made an eloquent plea for a greater ecclesiological self-understanding on the part of the various churches. This call for a clearer ecclesiology, that is, a systematic understanding of the nature and purpose of the Church, was a task Gabriel tackled in his book, *The Form of the Church* (Faber 1944). As far as Gabriel was concerned, the reunion of the churches ought not be regarded as a kind of ecclesial counter-part to the League of Nations, for the work of reunion was a theological task, and not simply a pragmatic occupation. So, taking his cue from Congar, Gabriel believed that what was required first and foremost was a theological understanding of the Church, and an understanding which would place the task of ecumenism not so much as an attempt to construct a monolithic structure around the existing diversity of churches, but as recognising and realising the given unity of Christian people. The unity, that is, which is consti-tuted in and through Christ in the sacramental actions of Baptism and Eucharist.

In a recent ecumenical study *Christians in Communion* (Mowbray, 1990) Paul Avis sets out a persuasive case arguing in support of the imperative of communion, including a eucharistic Communion for all baptised Christians. The line of argument followed in this book, and its helpful discussion of recent ecumenical documents and re-ports, is sufficient to convince the reader that the controversy over the question of open Communion in the 1930s belongs to a very different age than our own. The agenda, and the terms of the discussion might have changed, but it must be remembered that some of the points of a discussion can easily be lost and forgotten, and in this, as in every other aspect of the Christian enterprise, there can be no proper future without a past, and no real imagining of what might be, without a remembering of what has been. Gabriel, like many of his generation were concerned with the foundations of ecumenicity, and in our own times, when movement from one denomination to another is easier and more frequent, and in those situations, such as Local Ecumenical Projects where two, or sometimes more denominations are using the same building and liturgical space, it is crucial that the foundations of ecumenicity are firmly set and understood. In this, ecumenical theology should play a central role, and it is interesting to trace how the serious and deliberate theological voice of ecumenical debate, so strongly advocated by Gabriel in his article, 'Open Communion' has occurred, and continues, through such bodies as the Anglican-Roman Catholic International Commission (ARCIC) and the World Council of Churches (WCC). Indeed, the importance of the theological aspect of ecumenical dialogue has recently been underlined, and sharpened, by the searching analysis of Avis in his *Ecumenical Theology and the Elusiveness of Doctrine* (SPCK, 1986). Since the 1930s and 1940s, the ecumenical climate has changed considerably, and it would be foolish to ignore the recent history of this the ecumenical century. So to conclude this section, let us bring Gabriel's voice into dialogue with a contemporary ecumenical theologian and writer.

In his *Christians in Communion*, Paul Avis argues with considerable justification that Christian *koinonia*, (the strongest sense of 'communion') is that which a Christian enters at Baptism and so Baptism is a sufficient basis for eucharistic Communion between the churches. In general terms the outline of the argument is valid and attractive, but at the particular level, the level at which things are actually experienced and understood, the fact remains that individuals are initiated into the Church according to the rites of a particular denomination, and the rite of each church is shaped and informed by a whole cluster of doctrinal assumptions and liturgical practices which are peculiar to that church. In other words there is a real tension between the universal, (that all in Baptism are incorporated into Christ), and the particular, (that Baptism is the means whereby an individual is made a member of, and in time is formed by, a particular denomination). Furthermore, the fact remains that there are substantial differences between the churches. Given the pluriformity of the Church, it might be necessary to qualify Avis's conclusion and say that although Baptism is the highest common factor between Christians of different denominations, it might not necessarily provide a sufficient basis for intercommunion. In the last analysis, it seems as though a viable ecumenism can only be based on the widest possible model of the Church.

Towards an Ecclesiology

Ecumenical discussion has often presupposed a dichotomy between the historic structures of the empirical Church, and what is taken to be the substance of Christian life and faith. This approach has assumed that it is possible, and desirable to separate form and spirit, and to distinguish between the Church as she manifests herself in time and space, and her hidden inner meaning. In other words, it is the assumption that one can, and probably should, separate the kernel from the husk of the Church. The authentic Catholic approach, with its more integrated and inclusive basis, would resist such a procedure, and argue that the life and faith of the Christian could not be isolated, or abstracted, from the historic and empirical life of the Church, despite all its ambiguities, and sometimes glaring contradictions. This argument was carefully set out by Michael Ramsey in his *The Gospel and the Catholic Church* (Longmans, 1936), a classic of twentieth-century Anglican theology. Indeed, its enduring value as a resource for ecclesiological and ecumenical discussion is confirmed by the fact that a second edition was published some twenty years later in 1956.

Ramsey's book significantly redrew the ecclesiological map by harnessing the insights and procedures of the emerging school of biblical theology to a historical analysis of the origins and significance of the Church's structures and ordering of ministry and worship. The result is an impressive account of how the meaning of the Christian proclamation is yoked to the very structures of the Church, the historic threefold ministry and forms of liturgical worship. In this sense, the book was both Catholic and Evangelical, and the two outlooks were juxtaposed in such a way that the one informed and illuminated the other, and both were seen to be ultimately grounded in the incarnation, death and resurrection of Christ. In a succinct and strongly stated conclusion, Ramsey drew the implications of his study for the whole ecumenical process, and its goal of Christian reunion. With a clear vision of the unity which Christians have in Christ, and an informed and reasonable understanding of the present situation in which the churches found themselves, he argued that, '. . . there is no limit to what may be done through the sections of Christendom learning of one another's thought and ways and worship, and recovering within themselves those truths without whose recovery their schemes for unity can have no meaning. Wherever those who have thought little of the "the Gospel" return to it, and wherever those who have thought little of the "mystical Body" search for it within themselves – reunion draws nearer. Schemes for reunion may fail, and yet their failure may be no loss if men are thereby driven back to those issues of death and resurrection wherein the unity of God is found'. *The Gospel and the Catholic Church* p. 225.

Michael Ramsey wrote this book when he was sub-warden of Lincoln Theological College. Kelham was within easy reach of Lincoln, and throughout the period when Ramsey was writing the book, he seems to have been in close contact with Gabriel, and to have consulted him at the various stages of the book's composition. Indeed, Gabriel's help in this way was duly acknowledged by the author in the preface, where he thanks the 'Revd A.G. Hebert SSM, for criticism and encouragement at every stage of the writing of the book'.

At the centre of his treatment of the empirical church, Ramsey argued that episcopal ministry and sacramental worship were implicit in the earliest witness of the New Testament itself, and in a characteristic passage, he states that 'the impact of the Gospel moulds the form of the Church, and its order itself proclaims that the Christ has come in the flesh, and that his people are one family'.

Such a method of pegging an understanding of the Church, with its threefold ministry and ordered worship to the nascent Christian movement witnessed to in the New Testament, was later adopted by Gabriel when he began to explicate F.D.Maurice's view that the Church's ministerial orders and its ordered liturgical worship, were the empirical and earthly signs of the Kingdom of Christ, in his study, *The Form of the Church*, (Faber, 1944). Whereas Ramsey had taken the Paschal mystery of Christ's death and resurrection as the key for understanding both the origins and the continuing meaning of the Christian Church, Gabriel took the so-called four marks or characters of the Church, that is, its unity, holiness, catholicity and apostolicity, as enshrined in the credal formula, and in turn, attempted to show how these four aspects of the Church were rooted in the New Testament witness to God's work of salvation in Christ. In this way, and following Ramsey's methodological approach, Gabriel sought to demonstrate how the very form, or structure of the Church was congruent with the New Testament witness to the universal mission of Christ, and indeed, implicit in the very apostolic basis of the primitive Church.

However, the implications for the reunion of the churches, which Gabriel drew from his analysis, were rather more bold and direct than the kind of implications which had been drawn by Michael Ramsey in his study.

Gabriel had settled down to write this book during the Second World War. During that period, the student numbers at Kelham had dropped considerably, and there was, consequentially, more time for those who remained at the House for thinking, reading and writing. George Every, for instance, was busy building a bridge towards the orthodox east as he worked on his substantial study, published soon after the war and entitled *The Byzantine Patriarchate c451–1204)* (SPCK 1947). A contemporary church historian, writing on Christian attitudes to peace and war, has remarked on the irony of the fact that while Europe was locked in conflict, the English churches seemed to be absorbed in their own internal affairs, and their theologians preoccupied with what at the time seemed like trivia, namely, Church order and ministerial validity. In many respects the observation made by Alan Wilkinson can be justified, but in their defence, as it were, it must also be noted that for a number of theologians at the time, the question of the reunion of the churches was not divorced from a real concern for the unity and peace of the wider human society. A serious engagement with an understanding of the Church and the unity which Christ willed for his people, was clearly a sign of a wider commitment to the cause of peace and international understanding and co-operation. There were some, like Gabriel, who believed that Christian unity was an indispensable prerequisite for a lasting European peace, and this sentiment was clearly expressed in his *Unity in the Truth*, where he wrote, 'The reunion of our disintegrated civilisation . . . awaits the reunion of the Christian churches'. (p. 63)

So, there were many reasons which gave the task of constructing an ecclesiology a particular urgency and importance. On the whole, Gabriel's work in this regard was well received. William Temple, then Archbishop of Canterbury, wrote to Gabriel after he had read

The Form of the Church, expressing the fact that he was pleased that 'we are getting from you . . . a perfectly strong and clear presentation of the Catholic tradition which is at the same time sympathetic towards the Reformed churches and shows a real eagerness to understand them and to allow for the truth in their positive contentions'.[14] In a similar vein, Ramsey in a review of the book, described it as an uncompromising Catholic exposition of the nature of the Church. In the book, Gabriel had taken note of an earlier work, *The Nature of Catholicity*, (Faber, 1942), written by the Congregationalist scholar, Daniel Jenkins, and had sensitively handled Jenkin's critique of the Roman claims of supremacy. However, there is a note of defensiveness in Gabriel's treatment of the relationship between the apostolic nature of the Church and episcopacy. Here, he rehearsed the predictable catholic line that the apostolate instituted by Christ did not come to an end with the death of the original apostles, as some Protestant scholars argued that it did, but rather continued in and through the episcopal ministry of the early Church. Historically speaking, such a claim would be extremely difficult to substantiate, but Gabriel rehearses it here, and again, with an even greater confidence, in his essay, 'The Ministerial Episcopacy', which was published by Kenneth Kirk in *The Apostolic Ministry* (Hodder and Stoughton, 1946).

In 1945 an impressive gallery of Anglican theologians and Christian intellectuals of the 'Catholic' school of thought, which included V.A.Demant, Michael Ramsey, Austin Farrer, Lional Thornton CR, and Gabriel, was brought together, at the request of the Archbishop of Canterbury, to write a report on Catholicity. The report, *Catholicity: A Study in the Conflict of Christian Traditions in the West*, (Dacre, 1947), was published two years later, at the time when Catholic-minded Anglicans had their greatest influence upon the character and thought of the Church of England.

The Archbishop, Geoffrey Fisher, was anxious for the Church of England to seek a way through the apparent ecumenical deadlock, and looked to his report working party to provide a fair and thorough analysis of the causes and nature of the divided Church in the West. The proceedings of the working party were chaired by Michael Ramsey, who at that time was a professor of theology at Durham, and Gabriel and Dom Gregory Dix of Nashdom Abbey acted as secretaries. The final report offered an analysis of the three major traditions: (1) the Protestant traditions which had their roots in the Reformation; (2) the Liberal tradition, which was regarded as

having its heyday in the nineteenth century, but as having its anteced-
ents in the Renaissance tradition; and to complete the picture, (3) a
vignette of post-Tridentine Catholicism.

Gabriel, of course wrote well, and a great deal of the report issued
from his pen, but from the correspondance between the two secretaries, it is evident that Gabriel wanted to present the Protestant
traditions in a far more favourable light than his co-secretary.
Alongside the attempt to see divided Christendom in a historical
perspective, the report also offered a diagnosis of the current ecumenical impasse, and highlighted certain aspects of Anglican self-understanding, such as the notoriously vague notion of comprehensiveness,
which might possibly provide some points of orientation to steer the
ecumenical cause forward.

What was required at that stage, particularly in Anglo-Catholic
circles, was unwittingly suggested in the very title of the report,
namely a shift in attitude away from a narrowly defined catholicism,
to a more open and inclusive catholicity.

The truth of the matter is that Gabriel was detached from the
Anglo-Catholic attitude which was reinforced by a strongly-felt
conviction and all too often expressed in rather contentious argument. However, by 1947, when the Church of South India was fully
installed, the acrimony and threats which had issued from certain
quarters of the Catholic movement in the Church of England simply
withered away and were no longer heard, and some years later,
when Gabriel was based at St Michael's House, Adelaide, the SSM
theological college in Australia, he produced a second edition of *The
Form of the Church*. In the preface to this second edition, Gabriel
admits that his original chapter dealing with the theme of apostolicity, and particularly its discussion of episcopacy, had 'met with
severe criticisms from many of the reviewers; and it seems to me now
that these criticisms were largely justified, at least as regards the
manner in which I presented my argument'. (p. 9) In this same
preface, Gabriel states that his overall aim was to help and not
hinder the cause of Christian unity, and that in accordance with that
aim, the final chapter, dealing with apostolicity, had been completely
rewritten. In this chapter, Gabriel defines the episcopal office as
being something given, and as belonging to the essential form of the
Christian Church, and not simply a historical legacy, or option for
ecclesiastical organisation. In general terms, the episcopal office
represented a focus for the Church's unity and a continuity in the
exercise of its ministry. Thus he says, 'The episcopal office, inherited

from the undivided Church, is of its very nature a sacramental thing, an effectual sign of the unity of Christ with other bishops and their flocks in other places'.[15]

This statement echoes a point Gabriel had made during a discussion on the historic episcopate, at an official consultation of Anglican delegates who had attended the third international Faith and Order Conference at Lund, in August 1952. At this discussion, Gabriel had ventured the opinion that the Anglican Church had never in its history officially espoused, or enjoined upon its adherents, a single theory, or doctrinal understanding of episcopacy, and to argue in favour of the episcopacy as being of the essence of the Church would be incompatible with a spirit of theological repentence. Having made such a generous remark, however, he then went on to explain that he would not subscribe to a view of the historic episcopate, which saw it simply as a means of ecclesiastical government, and he offered the positive suggestion that what was required was a conception of the episcopate as a 'mysterium', that is, an indispensable part of the whole sacramental expression of the Christian life. Here indeed was a richly suggestive viewpoint, but one which he himself realised required further elaboration.

On the whole, it seems as though Gabriel never repented of the view that episcopacy was a living, visible and God-given sign of the unity and continuity of Christ's ministry in the Church, and so, even in his latter years when he happily conceded that non-episcopal ministries were real ministries of Christ's Word and Sacraments, he still maintained that the central problem in the process of the reunion of the churches, was the question of how episcopal and non-episcopal ministries might be reconciled and correlated in a united church.[16] Incidentally, it was precisely at this point that the Anglican-Methodist reunion scheme, so resolutely supported by Archbishop Michael Ramsey, floundered so disastrously some eight years after Gabriel's death, in July 1971.

In worship above all, the Church is seen to be what it is

As an Anglican, Gabriel's faith had been nourished and informed by what is essentially a liturgical Church, and this process had been reinforced by his membership of a religious community, whose common life was focused upon and driven by the full liturgical round of Church's daily prayer. Given this background, it was perhaps inevitable that his theological work, whether in the ecumenical field, or more particularly in his writings on the nature of the Church and the challenges of reunion, would be ultimately related to the Church's corporate and sacramental worship. Indeed, it seems as though there was a kind of gravitational pull in all his thinking and writing to the liturgical traditions of the Church, as if these provided the final reference point. Such an approach sprang from a deep-seated conviction, (one could almost describe it as the Anglican instinct), that worship was the definitive activity of the Church. As he repeatedly claimed, when the people of God gather for worship, the Church is clearly seen to be the Church.

It was appropriate, therefore, that one of Gabriel's most significant contributions to the ecumenical task of facilitating a greater under-standing between the churches should be concerned with the phenom-enon of worship.

The Second World Conference on Faith and Order, which met in Edinburgh in 1937, concluded that the most serious issues dividing Christians were directly related to worship, and in its final report the conference recommended that three theological commissions be set up to investigate respectively, 'the Church', 'Ways of Worship', and thirdly, the intractable problem of 'Intercommunion'. These three Commissions were appointed by the Continuation Committee of Edinburgh 1937, and each managed to hold one residential meeting before the proceedings were interrupted by the outbreak of the Second World War. The work of the second Commission, concerned with Ways of Worship, was resumed with a short residential meeting in 1947, and from then on, various papers from the individual members of the Commission were exchanged for criticism and com-ment. The Commission gathered again for a residential meeting in the summer of 1950, and the purpose of this meeting was to reach agreement on the final form of their report. By this time, it was intended that the reports of the three Commissions would provide the bulk of the preparatory material for the Third World Confer-ence on Faith and Order, which was planned to take place at Lund, in Sweden, in August 1952. Material from Gabriel was in-cluded in two of the final reports, *Intercommunion*, and *Ways of Worship*.

Ways of Worship (SCM 1951), was set out in three parts and provided a comparative study of the characteristic ways of worship of the different churches. The scope of the report was considerable and ranged across the whole spectrum of styles and patterns of worship from Roman Catholic and Orthodox through to an account of the meetings of the Society of Friends, so-called Quaker worship. The material was arranged in three parts and appeared under the headings of 'Elements of Liturgy', 'Inner Meanings of Word and Sacrament', and 'Liturgy and Devotion'. Gabriel's contribution to the final report was placed in the first part and sought to provide the Anglican perspective within that particular section. It was lucidly written and set out in a straightforward way an anatomy of worship, showing the various elements of Christian prayer, such as adoration, thanksgiving, penitence, and supplication, and offering an account of the ways in which Christian prayer was closely related to the regular and corporate Sunday celebration of the resurrection of the crucified Christ – a celebration, which according to this account, should exhibit a perfect balance of words and silence, song, movement and sacramental signs. Written within such a short compass of thirteen pages, the article still stands as an illuminating description of the essence and ethos of Anglican worship, and a clear summary of some important liturgical principles.

Horton Davies, the Congregationalist scholar and author of the five-volume work, *Worship and Theology in England* published in the early 1960s, claimed that Gabriel ought to be remembered above all for the ways in which he helped so many through his writing, teaching and personal example, to appreciate the singular importance and priority that worship should have for the community of faith. His most notable achievement in this respect was the way in which he introduced the insights and convictions of the Continental Liturgical Movement to the English churches through his *Liturgy and Society* (Faber, 1935). So, it comes as no surprise to discover in his article in 'Ways of Worship' a summary account and rehearsal of the primary ideals of that Movement, and the application of the term 'sacrifice' as the controlling metaphor of eucharistic worship. As we shall see in a further chapter, some of the theological thinking which undergirded the Liturgical Movement offered a reappraisal of the eucharistic doctrine of sacrifice, and spelt out an understanding of eucharistic sacrifice which some thought would circumvent the kind of doctrinal controversy which had divided the Church at the Reformation, and thereby open the way for some doctrinal rapprochement. Convinced by the theologians of the Liturgical Movement, particularly those associated with the Rhineland Abbey of Maria Laach, Gabriel consistently spoke of eucharistic worship as being essentially the means whereby the Christian community was associated with, and caught up in the offering of Christ to the Father.

In the final report of the third theological Commission 'Intercom-munion' Gabriel bravely attempts a more systematic account of eucharistic worship as sacrifice. Here, he carefully maps out the ground of his argument and deliberately clears the ground of any possible misapprehensions of the term. He admits that the term sacrifice was often taken as being a contentious term in theological argument, but he counters this with an impressive appeal to readers to appreciate that the term, far from denoting a narrow dogmatic assertion, was in fact a richly nuanced term, and one which properly expressed the inner meaning of eucharistic worship. Thus, Gabriel argues that the eucharistic sacrifice was not a re-immolation of Christ, nor a sacrifice added, as it were, to Christ's own sacrifice, but the divinely appointed means whereby the faithful might participate in, and receive the benefits of Christ's sacrifice on the cross of Calvary. To explain this mystery of Christian worship, Gabriel claims that 'The true celebrant is Christ the High Priest, and Christian people are assembled as members of His Body to present before God His Sacrifice, and to be themselves offered up in sacrifice through their union with Him'.[17]

In this article, entitled, 'A Root of Difference and Unity', Gabriel rather ambitiously sought to mediate a catholic understanding of sacrifice for the protestant reader. His method was to trace the notion of sacrifice back to the New Testament and to the Liturgies of the early Church, in the hope of demonstrating that this understand-ing of the Eucharist was compatible with the Pauline and Lutheran doctrine of justification by faith. Such an aim, of course, led him into the very centre of doctrinal controversy. A friend and eminent Swedish Lutheran theologian, Gustav Aulén found the general thrust of Gabriel's argument acceptable, but remained unconvinced by its details, and in his own later study *Eucharist and Sacrifice* (Muhlen-berg, 1956), he offers a critique of Gabriel's contribution to 'Intercom-munion'. Here, he applauds the genuineness of Gabriel's ecumenical motives. No one can deny, he says, that Hebert comes to his task in a truly ecumenical spirit, but what is implied and later shown, is that Gabriel failed to muster sufficient theological force to secure the acceptance of his conclusions. This criticism, however, was far from damning. On the contrary, Aulén welcomed the way in which Gabriel had spoken of the relationship between the Eucharist and the one, unrepeatable and sufficient sacrifice of Christ on Calvary, and particularly appreciated Gabriel's attempts to widen the vocabulary of sacrifice in speaking of the eucharistic oblation as a 'presenting

The Revd A. Gabriel Hebert, ssm
Visiting English Lecturer, Berkeley Divinity School,
Fall Term 1948–1949

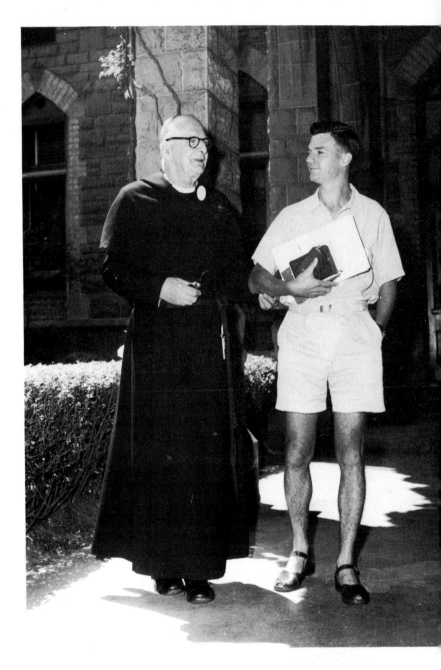

Gabriel Hebert at the first National Conference
of Australian Churches. Melbourne 2–11 February 1960

before God', and a 'pleading' before the Father of the 'one sacrifice of Christ'. Such a widening of the terms was clearly taken as a positive contribution to the theological debate, and one which held out the possibility of a greater ecumenical consensus.

However, for Aulén, as for many others, the real sticking point in the debate on eucharistic sacrifice, was the question of how and at which point in the eucharistic liturgy, the gathered worshipping community and its liturgical president could be said to make the eucharistic sacrifice. Thus he concludes his consideration of Gabriel's argument with the incisive judgement that 'There are reasons for saying that the sacrifice of Christ is present in the Eucharist, but none for saying that *we* offer this sacrifice'.[18]

At the Third World Conference on Faith and Order, at Lund, there were many who openly expressed their desire to see the mutual offering of eucharistic hospitality between the churches, but a study such as Aulén's *Eucharist and Sacrifice*, was ample testimony to the fact that the various churches affiliated to the World Council of Churches still had a considerable distance to cover in discussion and debate, before any agreement could be reached on what, in doctrinal terms, such eucharistic *koinonia* might entail. Even as late as 1962, Gabriel made it plain to an ecumenical graduate school at Bossey (the W.C.C's Ecumenical Institute near Geneva, in Switzerland) that Anglicans were not ready for intercommunion, and in that context, of course, that was a difficult and painful position to maintain. Nevertheless, Gabriel realised that there were various levels of participation, and in a popular book on the mission of the Church, written in 1958, he actively encouraged Christians not only to pray for each other, but to pray with each other, and to share in the worship of other churches and Communions. This he says is a positive sign within an empirically divided Church, which manifests the reality of that Christ-given unity which 'cannot be broken even by the divisions of the Churches', and in a characteristic passage, he continues '. . . prayer and worship are the points at which the Church is most clearly seen for what it is, and the Christians know what they are. True, we are divided in our worship; yet even so, when we grasp hold of the spiritual realities which the Signs signify, there is no reason why we should not, and every reason why we should, pray not only *for* our fellow Christians from whom we are separated, but also *with* them, joining in spirit in their prayer, and they in ours'.[19]

Having traced the development of Gabriel's ecumenical thinking, what can be said by way of conclusion? The first point to become evident is that with his ever widening circle of ecumenical contacts and involvements, Gabriel himself came to personify the principle of the catholicity of the Church, a a principle which he had learnt from his mentor Fr Kelly. In an often quoted letter of encouragement to a young brother of the Society, who was somewhat daunted by the enormity of the missionary task in South Africa, Kelly had written to the effect that it is impossible to make a Church out of denominations. This view certainly shaped the SSM approach to ecumenism, and Gabriel had consistently maintained that the goal of Christian unity was not the amalgamation of denominations, or even worse, the absorption of numerically smaller denominations to form a monolithic 'super-church', but rather, to quote some words from the *Catholicity* report, the 'recovery of the wholeness and unity given in Christ and his Church'. In other words, what was envisaged was not a universal assent and adoption of a set system of ecclesiastical belief and practice, (which in Kelly's view would only result in the creation of an 'ism'), but a common discovery of a conscious and living sense of the catholicity of the Church. Admittedly, the term catholicity is more elusive than the term catholicism, but it is derived from an appreciation of the character of God's dealings with humanity, which are always inclusive and universal in intention. If God is catholic, in this sense, then the Church too must be catholic, and her life and witness must be generously inclusive, accessible, and of universal application. This, for Gabriel was the heart of the matter, and its life-blood was the forward moving tradition of the historic three-fold ministry, established and expressed in the liturgical forms of the Church's worship. Gabriel's sense of the catholicity of the Church and his positive evaluation of tradition, which he would never have confused with traditionalism, led him to affirm the possibility that the Church could express and embody the plenitude of God's truth, but deny that that truth could be adequately set down in propositional form, or codified as the definitive and 'official teaching' of the Church.

At the beginning of the new academic year at St Michael's House, in 1960, Gabriel rather puzzled a group of new students by introducing himself as a retired Anglo-Catholic, but what he was really saying on that occasion was that through many years of prayer, study, and faithfulness to the best traditions of the SSM, he had come to appreciate and appropriate for himself a sense of the catholicity of the Church.

Secondly, it is beyond doubt that Gabriel, through his work and writing in England and later in Australia, came to be recognised as an ecumenical figure. In 1962, when Gabriel was seventy-six years of age and yet still displayed a youthful enthusiasm, he took part in the autumn term Graduate School at Bossey. This course was built around a theme which was very close to Gabriel's heart, 'Worship and Daily Life'. He had been asked to deliver four lectures, which followed an historical approach examining in turn, worship in the New Testament, worship in the Early Church, worship in the Middle Ages, and worship at the Reformation. Other lectures were given by two world-renowned ecumenical theologians, Professor Nissiotis, and Hans Rudi Weber. Apart from the formal lecturing, Gabriel was also asked to conduct a study group on prayer, and to act as chaplain to the Anglican participants. Regarding this latter responsibility, Gabriel offers an interesting vignette in a letter which he wrote to the recently elected Director of the SSM, Fr Gregory Wilkins. Here, he says: 'As for us Anglicans, we are having Mass on Sundays (with Mattins), and on Tuesdays and Thursdays, if those are suitable days in the week, in a lovely little chapel at the top of a low tower; one does various "advanced" things there, such as westward position, time for those present to mention special subjects for prayer before the Prayer for the Church; and at the end we all say the Prayer of Thanksgiving together. We Anglicans shall also be responsible for two weeks of the "Morning Prayers" in four weeks time, and for a Sunday morning. The Lutherans are doing this now and it is rather trying, for the American Lutheran Prayerbook has a sort of Mattins with Anglican chant à la Stainer!'

What was learnt at this Graduate School was not confined to the lecture room, or the discussion group, for much was gained from being part of a residential worshipping community, consisting of fifty students representing some twenty-one nations and fourteen denominations. The Graduate School was a truly international and ecumenical gathering, and within that setting Gabriel acted as an ecumenical go-between. His opinions were sought, and many responded warmly to his interest and natural friendliness. Kenneth Woolhouse, who was one of the Anglican students at the School, has said that he and the other Anglicans were proud to have Gabriel as the official Anglican representative, and that in that setting he had come across as a prophetic figure.

Despite the intensive programme at Bossey, and a ten-day spell in hospital in Geneva, due to a haemorrhage in the right eye, Gabriel managed to visit Grandchamp, a kind of sister community to the ecumenical community of brothers at Taizé, in France, and to spend two days at the Lutheran religious community for both women and men at Imshausen. He returned to Kelham on 18 December, and on his return confided in a brother that apart from fulfilling a couple of outside engagements, he wanted more than anything to spend his time, not writing, but thinking and praying; and given his recent completed itinerary, it would not be fanciful to imagine that a great deal of that praying centred around prayer for the unity of the Church in the fulness of Christ's truth.

Throughout the following year, Gabriel's health was unstable, and in July, having suffered a minor stroke, he was admitted to Newark hospital. He died in hospital on the 18th July 1963, and remarkably, an orbituary appeared the following day in the *Church Times*; a testimony in itself to the scale of Gabriel's influence, and the affection with which he was held in the wider church.

4
LITURGICAL RENEWAL

GABRIEL'S FIRST liturgical project was undertaken during his early years in South Africa. The Church of the Province of South Africa had come into being in 1870; and the first article of its Constitution not only affirmed the Province's reception and adhesion to the 1662 Book of Common Prayer, but also gave the necessary powers of 'any General Synod, Council, Congress or other Assembly of the Anglican Church' to make 'adaptions and abridgement of, or additions to, the services of the Church', and such powers opened the way for a thoroughgoing revision of the liturgy. In 1908 a Liturgical Commission was appointed, and after three years of deliberations and consultation, an official list of suggested variants from the standard 1662 Communion Office was published. During this time, unofficial and private proposals for a radically revised eucharistic canon were being canvassed. The issue which was being forced, was whether the 1662 Communion rite should be simply enriched, with the provision of additional material, or revised to the extent of being virtually rewritten. The issue was finally resolved in 1918 with the publication of the bishops' 'Proposed Form', which provided a restructured and extended eucharistic canon, authorised to be used experimentally. That same year a newly appointed Liturgical Commission widened the discussion of liturgical revision by opening up the question of the revision of the whole Prayer Book, and with regard to the needs of a largely missionary Church, proposed that steps might be taken to compile a new rite for the Christian initiation of adult converts.

In 1921, Fr George Carlton, the SSM Provincial in South Africa, suggested to Gabriel that he might attempt to compile a liturgical text for adult initiation, and if he was satisfied with the result, it could be sent to the Liturgical Commission for their consideration. In response to this suggestion, Gabriel drafted a series of texts which took adult initiation, rather than infant Baptism, as the norm of Christian initiation. The 1662 Book of Common Prayer had, of

87

course, included a service for the Baptism of those who were 'of riper years', but this text, which was included to meet the pastoral need of those who had not been baptised as infants during the time of the Puritan Commonwealth, and the slave workers engaged in England's foreign 'plantations', was modelled upon the infant baptismal rite. Gabriel's draft initiation services, on the other hand, envisaged the restoration of the adult catechumenate, which provided a staged process of Christian formation, marked with liturgical celebrations, and enabled adults to make the transition from life in a pagan society to the life of faith in the Body of Christ, in a way which gave them sufficient time to appropriate that faith for themselves and to feel that they indeed belonged to the community of faith. The catechumenate had been an institution of the early Church, which found itself in a religiously plural world, and so one in which the boundaries of the Christian society and the wider world had to be clearly marked and differentiated. Becoming a Christian demanded a change in life-style and a reordering of human aims and values. Significantly, others were involved in the process, so that the convert's journey of faith was always a shared journey. Mature Christians would act as sponsors, and some would fulfil the role of catechist, or teacher. This catechumenal process of Christian formation is fully described in the third-century document, the *Apostolic Tradition*, ascribed to Hippolytus of Rome, and the institution itself reached its full flowering in the fourth century, but thereafter soon disintegrated with the rapid expansion of Christianity, and the establishing of infant Baptism as the norm of Christian initiation.

Gabriel's motives in drawing upon the catechumenal model for his draft initiation services, did not spring from a desire to engage in some liturgical archeaology, but were prompted by his perception of a missionary situation in which large numbers of adults were seeking to convert to Christianity, and his own involvement in the SSM's work of training catechists at Modderpoort. Interestingly, the impetus for the restoration of the catechumenal model of Christian initiation within the Roman Catholic Church also came from the missionary territories in Africa. The Constitution on the Sacred Liturgy of 1963, endorsed the adult catechumenate as the classical model of Christian formation and prescribed the revision of the rites of Baptism for adults. Following this endorsement of the Second Vatican Council, the Rite for the Christian Initiation of Adults, (R.C.I.A.), was eventually produced and authorised for use in 1972. Subsequently, other Communions have begun to take an interest in the adult catechumenate, and of particular note is the Episcopal Church of the United States of America, whose *Book of Occasional Services*, (1979), provides some useful and well written liturgical material which might be used to mark and celebrate the various phases of the catechumenal process.

To return to the Anglican Province of South Africa, a serious commitment to meet the catechetical and liturgical needs of adults seeking Christian Baptism is reflected in the fact that their first Book of Common Prayer, published in 1954, contained a form for the admitting of catechumens. Lack of documentary evidence makes it difficult to estimate the degree to which Gabriel's proposed initiation services influenced the material which in time was included in the 1954 Prayer Book, but the form provided there for adult Baptisms, like Gabriel's proposals, is shorn of exhortatory material, and includes the two post-baptismal ceremonies of the Chrysom, the clothing of the newly baptised in a white garment, and the giving of a lighted candle. However, Gabriel's various proposals, which included 'A form for the Admission to Preparation for Baptism', 'The Order for the Baptism of Adults', 'The Order for the Baptism of Infants', and an 'Order for Confirmation', originally drafted in 1921, were published together, with the title *An Essay in Baptismal Revision*, in England by the Dacre Press in 1947, with the expressed intention that they might stimulate discussion within the Church on the theology and practice of the rites of Christian Initiation.

Prayer Book Revision

By the time that Gabriel returned to England, the Church of England was moving towards the final stages of its Prayer Book revision. The story of the Proposed Alternative Prayer Book of 1927 is a sad episode in the Church's history, and one which can be briefly told. The greatest contribution to the revision of the English Prayer Book was made by the distinguished liturgical scholar, Walter Frere, (1863–1938), one of the founding fathers of the Community of the Resurrection. As early as 1911, Frere had published *Some Principles of Liturgical Reform*, an important book which constructively tackled what an increasing number of people considered to be the urgent problem of liturgical revision. The Order for the Ministration of Communion provided in the 1662 Book of Common Prayer, the only authorised and canonical eucharistic rite in the Church of England, was increasingly regarded as being a deficient and unsatisfactory rite by those whose sacramental consciousness had been raised by the teaching of the nineteenth-century Tractarians. The most urgent need was seen to be the rearrangement of the eucharistic canon, and this need was forcefully put by Frere: 'It will probably be recognised that the present state of our liturgy at this point is gravely at variance, both with the oldest and most universal liturgical tradition, and also with the practical needs of today'.[1]

In February 1912, the Archbishop of Canterbury, Randall Davidson convened an Advisory Committee on Liturgical Questions, which included scholars such as Frere, F. E. Brightman and Percy Dearmer. Their work, of course, was interrupted by the First World War, 1914–1918, and the very horror and waste of those years seemed to shake the Church of England into a new awareness of the effectiveness of its mission. On the evidence of military chaplains and the YMCA, the Committee came to the conclusion that in England 'the instinct for worship has seriously diminished'. The result of such a religious stock-taking immediately after the war, was to intensify and make more urgent the task of liturgical revision. In the early 1920s, as a result of private initiative, three experimental Communion rites were published; the first, the so-called 'Green Book', produced by the English Church Union, appeared in 1922, and was closely followed by the 'Grey Book', the work of a more liberal group including Percy Dearmer and F. R. Barry, and finally, the 'Orange Book', which was largely the work of Frere. By this stage, (1923), Frere had been consecrated as Bishop of Truro. In part, his consecration to the episcopate was intended to add weight and influence to the work of liturgical revision, but ironically, his elevation to the bench of Bishops meant that as time went on and became more critical, Frere was often unable to attend liturgical conferences and revision committee meetings because of the pressure of diocesan engagements. One important example of this, was the second Farnham Conference, which took place from 28 to 30 April 1926. The first session of this crucial conference was devoted to a discussion on matters of eucharistic theology, specifically the eucharistic sacrifice, and 'consecration', and the second day was given over to discussion of a newly drafted eucharistic canon, drafted by R. G. Parsons, which it was thought might attract a more general approval than the two other competing drafts of the alternative canon. Parsons' text came to be known as the Farnham Canon, and followed the general lines which had first been proposed by Frere, with the Prayer of Oblation following immediately after the Institution narrative, and an Epiclesis, an invocation to the Holy Spirit written into the material following the Institution narrative. The structure of this Canon anticipated the kind of anaphoral, or eucharistic prayer, construction which was to become normative in the later revisions of the 1960s and 1970s. At the Farnham Conference, it was believed that the Epiclesis in Parsons' text was phrased in a more acceptable form than that in the two competing texts.

As we shall see, the Epiclesis proved to be one of the most contentious issues in the alternative Communion rite in the proposed 1927 Prayer Book. In this text, the invocation to the Holy Spirit was placed after the Institution narrative, (where it was found, and continues in the eucharistic prayers of the Scottish Episcopal Church), and its final phrasing was the work of the then Archbishop of York, Cosmo Gordon Lang. In the prayer, addressed to the Father, a petition was made in such a way that it begged the question as to whether the Holy Spirit was the agent, or the instrument of consecration: 'Hear us, O merciful Father, we most humbly beseech thee, and with thy Holy and Life-giving Spirit vouchsafe to bless and sanctify both us and these thy gifts of Bread and Wine, that they may be unto us the Body and Blood of thy Son, our Saviour Jesus Christ, to the end that we, receiving the same, may be strengthened and refreshed both in body and soul'.

Frere, in wanting to secure the general approval of the alternative Communion rite and to preserve the unity of the Church of England, suggested that the Epiclesis clause might be printed as an alternative option, but this expediency was rejected by his fellow bishops, who being so wedded to a literal view of 'common prayer', could not accept the idea of an optional variant within an alternative rite. So, at the end of March, 1927, when the Alternative Prayer Book was brought to Convocations, his support was not totally wholehearted. Nevertheless, despite his real concern over the Anglo-Catholic opposition to the inclusion of an Epiclesis, Frere publically supported the book and spoke in its favour. In the the event, the book was approved by large majorities in both Convocations of York and Canterbury. The second stage was its discussion in the newly formed Church Assembly, and at its meeting on 6 July, the voting on the Alternative Book was passed with a large majority of 79 per cent. There then followed a five month interval before the Measure to allow and authorise the book was to be brought before Parliament. This interval gave the opponents of the book, both Anglo-Catholics who claimed that the revision of the eucharistic rite had not gone far enough in a Roman direction, and the Evangelicals who felt that the reform had gone too far, time to organise their opposition and stir controversy. The fate of the book in the hands of Parliament is well known. In December after a three day debate, the Prayer Book Measure was passed with a substantial majority in the House of Lords, but met with defeat in the House of Commons, where the Measure was rejected by 238 votes to 205. The result was disheartening, and the Archbishops were determined not to acquiesce, or to effectively lose what amounted to twenty years' work of liturgical revision. So, the book was brought back to the Church Assembly in April 1928, in order that the necessary amendments to mollify its opponents could be made. A number of modifications were agreed and made, but the Epiclesis clause in the eucharistic prayer remained in-tact. On 13 June 1928, the Measure returned to Parliament, and after two days of heated debate, suffered an even greater defeat. A month later the bishops met and unanimously supported the strongly worded statement of the Archbishop of Canterbury that the Church, 'that is, the bishops together with the clergy and laity, must in the last resort, when its mind has been fully ascertained, retain its inalienable right to formulate its Faith ... and to arrange the expression of that Holy Faith in its forms of worship.' The bishops were in a strident mood, and there were murmurs of disestablishment, even from that most Erastian of bishops, Hensley Henson, but in the end, the status quo was maintained, and at the end of the year the so-called privileged presses were instructed to publish the 1928 Prayer Book, bearing the ambiguous caveat that 'The publication of this book does not directly, or indirectly imply that it can be regarded as authorised for use in churches.'

At Kelham the alternative canon in the 1928 Prayer Book was not generally accepted, and in 1933 a Kelham revision came into use. This was essentially a composite rite, made up from material from the alternative order in the 1928 Prayer Book, such as the Prayer for the Church, and the Farnham Canon, with its extended anamnesis, or commemoration, which rehearsed the resurrection and ascension of Christ as well as his suffering and death. This Kelham revision followed the order of the 'Interim Rite', which tacked the Prayer of Oblation, (said audibly after the Institution narrative), and the Lord's Prayer, onto the Prayer of Consecration. Herbert Kelly, ardently loyal to the liturgical forms 'authorised and allowed by canon', objected strongly to the Kelham usage, and would show his disapproval, in a characteristically attention-seeking way, by noisily shuffling out of Chapel as soon as he had received his communion. According to George Every, Kelly had been one of the few priests in the SSM who had approved of the alternative order of Holy Communion in the 1927 Prayer Book, and had been saddened by its fate.

As we have already indicated, the controversy over the alternative canon in the 1927/8 Prayer Book centred upon the epiclesis, the invocation of the Holy Spirit. For Anglo-Catholics this was a real stumbling-block. It was not that they simply objected to an epiclesis as such, (indeed, a weak form of epiclesis had been incorporated into the 'Green Book'), but to its position, being placed after the Institution narrative. This position was interpreted as effecting a serious break with the perceived western tradition of eucharistic prayer construction, as shown in Roman, Lutheran and Anglican forms. Historically the epiclesis had originated with the primitive practice of calling the divine name upon designated material objects in order to bless them, and set them apart for a holy use. After the Council of Nicea, AD 325, with the promulgation of a more defined trinitarian understanding of God, the epiclesis came to be more narrowly associated with the Holy Spirit. An explicit consecratory epiclesis was first expounded in the the fourth century by Cyril of Jerusalem in his catechetic lectures, and became a feature of the Byzantine liturgies of St Basil, and St John Chrysostom. In these Eastern liturgies we find a petition invoking the Holy Spirit to 'make', or 'change', the bread and wine into the Body and Blood of Christ, and this consecratory epiclesis is placed after the rehearsal of the Institution narrative and anamnesis, or commemoration of Christ's saving work.

The Anglo-Catholic opponents of the 1927/8 Prayer-Book regarded the epiclesis as a foreign insinuation into the eucharistic canon. Ironically though, the 1927 position of the epiclesis in the eucharistic prayer entered into the Prayer Book of that most 'Catholic' of Anglican Provinces, the Province of South Africa. The Anglo-Catholic opponents to the inclusion of an epiclesis in the eucharistic prayer, in both England and South Africa, rested their case on the grounds of the history of Western sacramental theology. Since the late twelfth and early thirteenth centuries, with the formulation of precisely defined eucharistic doctrine, the Western Church had identified the consecration of the elements with the recital of the dominical words, 'This is my Body', 'This is my Blood', in the Institution narrative. These words, spoken over the elements, provided a 'moment of consecration', a moment which was ritually heightened at the celebration of High Mass with the elevation of the elements – the showing of the sacrament to the people, the incensation and the ringing of bells. Such a devotional practice and doctrinal understanding produced the kind of mind-set which read the epiclesis in the 1927 alternative canon as a compromise, or even a denial of the traditional Western understanding of consecration. Thus for those who had been nurtured by Catholic doctrine and ritual, the notion of consecration, and the sacramental presence of Christ was at the heart of the matter.

Walter Frere had long contended that the Prayer of Consecration in the 1662 Prayer Book had unintentionally heightened and encouraged an understanding of a 'moment of consecration', by ending as it did with the people's 'Amen' immediately after the Institution narrative. This, Frere thought, was quite undesirable for a Church which regarded itself as being Catholic, but not Roman.[2] Gabriel Hebert's appreciation of the situation was close to Frere's, but in his case, he had been influenced by the Swedish theologian, Brilioth. In Brilioth's analysis, set out in his *Eucharistic Faith and Practice*, the Catholic Church had limited the mystery of the Eucharist by its exclusive concern with notions of consecration and the real presence. Thus Gabriel came to realise that a great deal of the dissatisfaction felt at the 1927/8 Prayer Book resulted from a narrow view of eucharistic consecration, and so he set out to discover a mediating position.

In an article entitled 'The Meaning of the Epiclesis', published in 1933 in the journal *Theology*, Gabriel addressed the problem and offered a possible solution by giving due weight to the consecratory function of the dominical words, and, at the same time, offering a positive account of the role of the Holy Spirit in the Eucharist. In this article he claims that the need for a revised eucharistic canon was 'extraordinarily urgent', and admitted that the epiclesis in the 1927 canon had been the real stumbling-block. He was convinced, however, that a revised canon 'must certainly contain an epiclesis', and based his following argument on an analogy with the doctrine of the atonement. He asserted that as the doctrine of the atonement needed to balance the salvivic work of Christ, the High Priest, with the work and operation of the Holy Spirit, so a similar balance had to be expressed in the wording of the eucharistic prayer. In terms of the Eucharist, the work of Christ and that of the Holy Spirit can be distinguished. Christ, he says, is properly regarded as the celebrant of the Eucharist, pleading his sacrifice to the Father and uniting his people to his own sacrifice. It is the Holy Spirit, on the other hand,

who consecrates the earthly elements, and in the hearts of the
faithful unites them with Christ, and brings forth in them the fruits
of the Spirit, making their lives an offering to God. According to
Gabriel's logic, the liturgical corollary of this doctrinal understanding, was that an adequate alternative eucharistic canon required a
full anamnesis, and a full epiclesis. Furthermore, he added the caveat
that the form of the epiclesis should be such as would 'preserve the
consecratory character of the Dominical Words'. What he was pleading for in this article was not a fudged compromise, but a eucharistic
prayer so framed as to give full justice to both the supposed Western
and Eastern traditions of eucharistic praying. The conclusion of the
article focuses more specifically upon the composition of the 1927
alternative canon, and suggests that the difficulty posed by the
position of the epiclesis in that canon could be resolved by framing a
double epiclesis, with the first petition, invoking the Holy Spirit to
sanctify the bread and wine, being placed *before* the institution
narrative, thus:

> Hear us, O merciful Father, we most humbly beseech
> thee, and with thy Holy Spirit vouchsafe to bless and
> sanctify these thy creatures of bread and wine according to
> our Saviour Jesus Christ's holy institution, who in the same
> night that he was betrayed . . .',

and the second petition, following the anamnesis, thus:

> And we beseech thee to pour thy Holy and life-giving Spirit
> on us and on thy whole Church, that all who are partakers
> of this holy communion may be fulfilled with thy grace and
> heavenly benediction, and be made one body with thy Son
> . . . that he may dwell in us and we in him'.

Gabriel's proposal here would certainly have dealt with some of
the difficulties which some people saw in relation to the 1927 Prayer
Book canon, and further, would have given the epiclesis, as a feature
of eucharistic praying, a fuller and more adequate expression.

However, at the time when Gabriel's article was published, certain
Anglo-Catholics were marshalling their arguments. In March 1934,
Gregory Dix published an article in *Theology*, 'The Origins of the
Epiclesis', which was a scholarly detailed, but polemical piece of
writing directed against those whom he pejoratively described as 'the
orientalizing school of liturgists'. In Dix's view, their historical
analysis appeared 'arbitrary and even unnatural when the evidence is

considered as a whole'. Gregory Dix, who for some years had struggled with the personal question of whether he ought to become a Roman Catholic, was wanting to defend what was considered to be the classical Western understanding of eucharistic consecration, and in his article he indulged in a certain amount of special pleading. Nevertheless, the scope of the evidence he adduced to support his argument was impressive. He argued that the Western tradition of eucharistic consecration, which dated back to Ambrose of Milan, of regarding the dominical words as being consecratory, was not only the generally accepted view, but also the most primitive.

Some years later, Gabriel took up the issue again in an article entitled, 'Anaphora and Epiclesis',[3] and as in his earlier article, sought to establish some common ground in what continued to be a polarised debate between what he styled as the 'Words theory' and the 'Spirit theory' of consecration. It was, as he correctly argued, the 'Words theory' in the Western Church which had posited the notion of a moment of consecration, and it was this latter and questionable notion which needed elucidation, or as we might put the matter more sharply today, demystification. Gabriel begins his article by paying tribute to Walter Frere for his eirenical study *The Anaphora or Great Eucharistic Prayer* (SPCK 1938), and suggests that the underlying key to the debate about the forms of the eucharistic prayer, was the meaning of the notion of consecration. Consecration, Gabriel argued, needed to be seen in the context of the whole eucharistic action; an action, which he conceived in terms of a dynamic interaction and exchange of things earthly and heavenly. In the Eucharist, the divine and eternal dimension intersects, as it were, the empirical dimension of the gathered church, as the Church's offering is joined to the one sacrifice of Christ, who ever lives to make intercession for us in the heavenly places. Alongside this view of a double action, Gabriel adds a similar notion of a double movement, an ascent and a descent. The ascent is seen in terms of God receiving the offering of his people, and the descent is seen as the 'heavenly benediction and grace' which is enjoyed by those who receive the divine gifts in Communion. The aspect of a double action, in his view, was supremely expressed in the anamnesis, and the double movement was best expressed in the eucharistic epiclesis. Such a double movement, he claimed, was at least implicit in the major eucharistic prayers of both east and west, and held in the closest tension. Thus he concludes that what lies behind the notion of consecration, is the joining of the heavenly reality with the

Church's material offering of bread and wine, and it is precisely at this point, he says, that 'we have the essential idea of the epiclesis of the Holy Spirit.'

In the end, Gabriel was vindicated, and the kind of views he was tentatively sketching for the readers of *Theology* became the general accepted views. The Second Vatican Council instructed those charged with the responsibility of composing new eucharistic prayers to be used as alternatives to the Roman Canon, to draw upon the full and authentic traditions of eucharistic praying, and the Consilium included a divided epiclesis in the *ingenium romanum*, the index of what is required to be included in the composition of a eucharistic prayer. Furthermore, recent Anglican and Free Church revisions of the eucharistic prayer have also tended to give some expression to the role of the Holy Spirit in the Eucharist, and this feature of contemporary eucharistic prayers has undoubtedly enriched the eucharistic praying of the Church, and has also had an important ecumenical significance. This ecumenical import was duly recognised in the Faith and Order Paper No.111 (1982), of the World Council of Churches, *Baptism, Eucharist and Ministry*, which includes the epiclesis in its taxonomy of the Eucharist.

A distinguished Orthodox theologian and liturgist, Alexander Schmemann in a recent study *The Eucharist*, (St Vladimir's Press, 1988), has convincingly shown that the scholastic legacy of seeking to tie the eucharistic consecration to a particular formula and locate its precise cause was not only unnecessary, but also quite harmful. The present consensus view is that it is the *whole* eucharistic prayer which is consecratory, and not solely one part of it. Furthermore, Schmemann argues that consecration is best understood as the transfiguring of the earthly with the heavenly, the meeting of time and eternity, a view which the perceptive reader will recognise as being similar in both vocabulary and logic to the underlying notion of consecration proposed by Gabriel Hebert in his article 'Anaphora and Epiclesis'.

Liturgical Renewal

Following the debacle over the 1927/8 Prayer Book, Gabriel's greatest-achievement was to break through the impasse of liturgical revision by providing, particularly through his *Liturgy and Society* (Faber, 1935), the impetus and agenda for liturgical renewal. The source and inspiration for such renewal was drawn from the

twentieth-century Liturgical Movement, which was burgeoning in
the Continental Roman Catholic Church, and from Brilioth's ecumenically sensitive study of eucharistic faith and practice. The attention
of English readers had first been drawn to the Liturgical Movement
by an article by F. Gavin in the November issue of *Theology*, 1929,
entitled 'Contemporary Religion in Germany'. This article included a
brief outline of the aims of the Movement, and an illuminating
account of the work of the Rhineland Benedictine Abbey of Maria
Laach. Gabriel himself did not visit the Abbey until 1932, but his
first contact with the Movement was through a young priest called
John Perret. Perret was of French extraction and had been ordained
as a Roman Catholic priest in 1921. On 10 October 1928, he was
received into the Church of England by the Bishop of London. He
then spent some time at Kelham, in order to absorb something of the
Anglican ethos and to acclimatise himself to Anglican ways. At
Kelham, Perret, who was once described by Maurice Reckitt as 'a
foremost authority on the Liturgical Movement', was befriended by
Gabriel, and the two men became life-long friends. In the early 1930s
Perret contributed a series of articles to the newly launched and
broadly socialist based journal, *Christendom*. In his first article,
which appeared in the December issue of 1932, Perret reviewed
Romano Guardini's book *The Spirit of the Liturgy*. Guardini had
been associated with Maria Laach, and the book had been written in
collaboration with the monks there, and was originally published in
1918 as the first volume of their series *Ecclesia Orans*. Perret's second
piece in *Christendom* was a contribution to an article entitled 'The
Next Hundred Years of Catholic Revival', which explored the future
possible directions of catholic thinking and practice in the Church of
England. This article introduced readers to the innovations of the
Liturgical Movement, and John Perret indicated certain parallels
between the endeavours of those who were leading the Movement,
and the leaders of the earlier nineteenth-century Oxford Movement
within the Church of England. Both Movements had strong intellectual leadership, and were fired by the same central conviction,
namely that the Eucharist should occupy the very centre of Christian
worship and the life of faith. Perret's third article in *Christendom*,
'The Significance of the Liturgical Movement',[4] gave a fuller account
of the main themes and objectives of the Movement. The very fact
that Perret's articles were published in *Christendom* is a good illustra-
tion of the conscious desire on the part of those who were caught up
in the Movement, to draw out the social implications of the Church's

worship. In his first article he confidently asserts that 'the Liturgical Movement could help towards the solution of the problem raised more than once by the writers of Christendom as regards the intimate relationship between worship and social action'. (vol.11 No.8, Dec. 1932, p.296). With such an expectation, it is not surprising that Gabriel chose for his book, originally conceived as 'a treatise on the principles of Christian worship, inspired to a large extent by the Liturgical Movement',[5] the simple title 'Liturgy and Society'. In Gabriel's case, however, it is likely, as has been suggested by Fr Antony Snell, that his notions of society were as much influenced by T.S. Eliot, who during the 1930s was a regular visitor to Kelham, and was at that stage beginning to shape his own views of a Christian society, as by Fr Reginald Tribe, the Director of the SSM, who was closely associated with the Christendom Group, and was one of the founders of the Anglo-Catholic Summer School of Sociology.

The Continental Liturgical Movement

The term 'Liturgical Movement' was first coined by Dom Prosper Gueranger, the Abbot of the French Abbey of Solesmes in the mid-nineteenth century. Solesmes became famous for its work in restoring Gregorian chant, but on the whole their concerns were somewhat introverted and ultramontane in attitude. It was in the early years of the twentieth century that the movement found its most authentic expression, and its centre shifted to another Benedictine monastery, albeit of the same Congregation, Mont Cesar in Belgium. This twentieth century expression of the movement was focused on Lambert Beauduin, a monk of Mont César, and its beginnings can be traced back to September 1909, when Beauduin spoke at a conference at Malines, the occasion being the celebrated fifth Congres National des Oeuvres Catholiques. At this conference Beauduin read a short paper, entitled 'La vraie prière de l'église', which was placed in a section which dealt with other contributions concerning liturgy and music. On the conference programme this section was curiously headed 'literary, artistic and scientific works', but Beauduin's paper was really a call to action, and was delivered as a manifesto. His address began by quoting some words of Pope Pius X, from his 1903 encyclical, 'Loto Proprio': '. . . the first and indispensable source of the true Christian spirit is to be found in the active participation of the faithful in the liturgy of the Church'. These words were to become the motto of the Movement, and 'participation' its watch-word. At the conference, however, Beauduin was not a single and isolated voice. One of the main papers was given by the historian Godefroid Kurth. Beauduin had been in correspondence with Kurth prior to the conference, and had managed to convey to him something of his conviction that the faithful needed to be encouraged and enabled to play a full part in the Church's liturgy. Kurth was clearly sympathetic to Beaudin's views, and in his own address, which was quoted in a local newspaper, declared that, 'The liturgy is the supreme summit of poetry and thought . . . On the day when the holy missal will stop being for many an unintelligible book, on that day when all will find again the key to what the priest says to God at the altar, a great number of those who have deserted the temples will return to them.'[6]

In this address, Kurth was addressing a situation of religious indifference, which was a consequence of increasing materialism and secular ideology, and clearly signalled the need for the mass to be translated into the vernacular. Beauduin was convinced that if the people could understand what was being said at the mass, then they would be able to enter more fully into the Church's prayer, and actually pray the mass, rather than use it as an occasion in which to make their own private devotions. For this reason, the issue of using the vernacular at the mass, was a priority on Beauduin's agenda for liturgical renewal. Beauduin's singular commitment to the cause of the renewal of the liturgy was, to a considerable extent, motivated by his pastoral awareness and experience. Prior to his becoming a Benedictine monk, Beauduin had spent some eight years living and ministering to factory workers and their families in the industrial area of Liege. For them, the worship of the Church, literally con-ducted in a foreign language, was an alien and alienating phenom-enon. One of the direct consequences of the Malines conference in 1909, was the production of Sunday mass texts, giving the readings and propers in both French and Flemish, for use in local parishes. The work of preparing and printing these notes was undertaken by the monks of Mont César, and by the summer of 1910, they were printing some 70,000 copies per week, for use in parishes throughout Belgium.

Thus the abbey of Mont César came to be seen as the centre of liturgical renewal and education. Regular liturgical study days were arranged at the abbey, and a monthly clergy review, aiming to renew the Church's liturgical life at the parochial level, was published in both French and Flemish. The review, edited by Beauduin, was deliberately a popular, rather than a scholarly journal, and the various articles sought to explain in straightforward terms the various aspects of the liturgy, to stress the importance of homilies, and to emphasise the need of the laity to be more participative, especially by making their Communion at the proper point in the mass, and not, as the general custom was, to receive Communion from the tabernacle immediately after the mass itself.

Unfortunately, the initiatives for liturgical renewal taken at Mont César were soon abruptly halted with the outbreak of hostilities in Europe in 1914. At that time Beauduin became actively involved in the German resistance, and also began to make contacts with Ortho-dox Christians, and members of the Ukrainian church, contacts which were to have a radical effect on the future direction of his work. These contacts with Byzantine rite Christians and his deep ecumenical vocation led, in 1926, to the establishing of a bi-ritual monastery at Amay. That eventful year also saw the publication of his book *La Piété de L'Eglise*, in which he set out the rationale and aims of the Liturgical Movement. The underlying theme of the book was the close connection between liturgy and life, and the exposition of this vital theme revolved around two theological poles. The first concerned the mystery of the incarnation, of God taking human nature in Christ and thereby entering into solidarity with the condi-tions of human life. This was regarded as a foundational theological datum, and one which provided the basis from which Beauduin could claim the divine affirmation of human dignity. The second theological pole in Beauduin's argument was an ecclesiological one, and focused on the Church as the society of the people of God, and the mystical Body of Christ, sacramentally present in and for the contemporary world. Beauduin laid considerable stress upon the corporate nature of the Church, as opposed to a congregational view, which might see the gathered Church as a local aggregation of individuals. This emphasis was a deliberate attempt to correct the kind of individualism, and its religious concomitant, subjective piety, which Beauduin felt was endemic in the Church. Needless to say, for Beauduin, these two theological convictions were no mere theoretical considerations, but were vital truths which enlivened the authentic liturgical experience of the Church. For when the people of God gathered to make Eucharist, they were reconstituted as the Church in that place, and associated with Christ's offering of himself to the Father, for the salvation of the world. So, the overall impression given by this book is that the worship of the Church must always be directed towards God, focused upon the person and salvivic work of Christ, but can only be adequately understood when it is considered in terms of both the corporate nature of the Church, and the real needs and aspirations of the wider human society in which the Church is set and to which she is called to minister, as the bearer of hope, and the catalyst in the process of making a more humane society. Liturgy and society, it seems, are inextricably bound together.

After the 1914–18 war, the centre of liturgical renewal shifted to the abbey of Maria Laach. Under the leadership of Ildefons Herwegen, abbot of the community from 1913 to 1946, Maria Laach became the place where the theological thinking of the Liturgical Movement found its most systematic analysis and presentation. At Maria Laach, Gavin found what he considered to be the full flowering of German Catholicism, and argued that on account of the depth and seriousness of its scholarship, the Liturgical Movement could not be accused of being archeological, of simply wanting to restore what was considered to be the ancient liturgical practice of the Church.[7] Apart from its scholarly work in the field of liturgical theology, the abbey soon gained the reputation of being a centre for liturgical renewal because of the various opportunities it gave to both clergy and laity to learn more about the Church's prayer and to participate more fully and consciously in its own rich liturgical life. During Holy Week 1914 was hosted its first liturgical week for laity, an occasion in which westward celebration of the mass was explained and demonstrated, and the dialogue mass, in which what was said in Latin by the priest and server in the sanctuary, was said aloud in German by a Vorbeter and the congregation in the pews, became an important means of liturgical catechesis.

As has already been indicated, the abbey at Maria Laach became renowned for the liturgical theology which was being written by its abbot, and Dom Odo Casel, (1886–1948). The abbot, Herwegen, was a prolific writer and his book *Kirche und Seele* was to be extensively quoted by Gabriel in his own *Liturgy and Society*. In *Kirche und Seele*, Herwegen advanced his opinion that the late Middle Ages was an era of liturgical corruption, because of the proliferation of private masses which it encouraged. In his reading of the situation, it was precisely the practice of private masses which had engendered the individualistic and subjective piety that had damagingly insinuated itself into what he believed ought to be an objective and essentially corporate liturgical celebration. The consequences of the private mass had distorted the Church's liturgy, and the undue emphasis upon the mass as the work of the priest had deprived the people of God from taking their proper place in the Church's worship. Herwegen was anxious to restore to the baptised people of God their proper participation in the liturgical action of the Eucharist, and to make the mass a 'sacrificial communion', and not solely an occasion for receiving sacramental benediction. He was also concerned to restore the balance of Word and sacrament in the Eucharist, and so he insisted that the vivifying Word of God was proclaimed in the biblical readings and sermon of the synaxis, as well as in the Verbum visible of the sacrament itself.

In Austria the aims of the Liturgical Movement were taken up and promoted at parish level by the Augustinian friars of Klosterneuberg. Here the central figure was Pius Parsch. He became the editor of an influential journal *Bibel und Liturgie*, and was applauded by Gabriel in *Liturgy and Society* for being one of the pioneers in the Continental Roman Catholic Church, who helped people to take the Bible seriously and to engage with the question of its place and function in the Church's liturgy.

Returning to Maria Laach, we can see that the cause of liturgical renewal was being well served by the deliberate intellectual efforts which were being made there to construct a liturgical theology which would undergird the cause. The kind of liturgical theology which was forged there, came to be known as 'Mysterientheologie', literally, mystery theology, and found its first exposition in Abbot Herwegen's *Kirche und Seele*, published in 1928. This Mysterientheologie was a theological construction which attempted to show how the whole saving work of God in Christ was made present to and for the worshippers in the liturgical action of the Church. This view recovered the wholeness of liturgical celebration, and argued that the saving work of God became *physically* present in the liturgical celebration to such a degree as to affect those who participated in the work of worship. This model of what was happening in the sacramental theatre was developed by a monk of Maria Laach, Dom Odo Casel (1886–1948) in the various writings he produced while he was the spiritual director to the Benedictine nuns of the Beuron Congregation, at the Abbey of the Holy Cross at Herstelle. The sisters of the community at Herstelle were largely responsible for the collation and publication of Casel's writing, most of which have not yet been translated into English. In terms of liturgical theology, Casel's most suggestive writing was set out in *Das Christliche Kultmysterium* in which he showed how the mystery of salvation history, focused in the incarnate life, death, resurrection and glorification of Christ, was dynamically re-presented in the worship of the Church and made accessible to its participants. This book, published by Casel in 1932, did not appear in English translation for another thirty years, when it appeared with the apt title *The Mystery of Christian Worship* (DLT, 1962). However, English readers were first acquainted with the model of Mysterientheologie, and its central concept of Gegenwartigzung, (literally, the 'making present' of that mystery spoken of in the deutero-Pauline epistles, in Ephesians 1:9 '. . . the mystery of his will, . . . which he set forth in Christ as a plan for the fulness of time, to unite all things in him,' and in Colossians 1:26f. '. . . the mystery hidden for ages and generations but now made manifest to the saints . . . Christ in you, the hope of glory.') through Gabriel's citations of Abbot Herwegen's work. Indeed, the chapter entitled 'Liturgy' in *Liturgy and Society*, opens with the following quotation from *Kirche und Seele*, where Herwegen argues that the mystery of salvation impinges upon the worshippers in the celebration of the mysteries, the sacramental worship of the Church, and that it is precisely the act of worship which is constitutive of the Church:

> 'Mystery in its general sacral sense is the re-presentation (Gegenwartigsetzung) of the salvation myth on which is based the existence of the cult-community which meets for the celebration of the mysteries. Similarly, the Christian Mystery is the re-presentation of the saving work of Christ, on which the existence of his Church is based'. (*Liturgy and Society*, p. 64)

Odo Casel's scholarly account of the Christian mystery was critically evaluated by the French liturgist Louis Bouyer in his *Life and Liturgy* (English translation, Sheed and Ward, 1956), and Bouyer convincingly demonstrates that Casel over-played his hand in drawing too close an analogy between the the pagan mystery cults and the liturgical rites of the primitive church. But far from wanting to jettison the central tenets of Mysterientheologie, Bouyer confidently set out to correct certain aspects of Casel's argument in the light of more recent critical study, and asserts 'Dom Casel's theory will emerge more clearly, and more securely established than before'. (*Life and Liturgy*, p. 98) The theory had certainly been welcomed in ecumenical circles. The World Council of Churches' Faith and Order

Report, 'Ways of Worship' (SCM, 1951), held out the hope that the liturgical theology propounded by Herwegen and Casel might provide the necessary common ground for a reapproachment of Catholic, Orthodox and Reformed views of the Eucharist. Its ecumenical potential was spelt out in these terms,

> 'This theology (of Maria Laach) contains great possibilities for future development and perhaps opens up the most promising approach to some understanding between the Roman Catholic and non-Roman Catholic churches'. (Ways of Worship, p. 33)

The model of liturgical theology proposed by Herwegen and Casel continues to be expounded today by Dom Burkhard Neunheuser, again a monk of Maria Laach, who in his own teaching and writing has drawn from the model of Mysterientheologie and proposed ways of understanding the sacraments, primarily as God's epiphanous action, rather than narrowly being 'a means of grace', and thereby contrasts sharply with those accounts of the sacraments which are framed in terms of the static and abstract categories of scholastic thought, or the more personalist and existential models suggested by the Catholic theologian Edward Schillebeeckx.

On the question of the development of Mysterientheologie, it ought to be noted that as a teacher and student of biblical studies, Gabriel Hebert was able to combine the dynamic understanding of the biblical notion of 'memorial' with the mystery theology of Maria Laach, and this he did with great effect in the talks and conference papers he wrote and delivered in the 1940s and 1950s. From a theoretical point of view these two conceptions, the one biblical and the other theological, were highly compatible, and in fact, provide a more adequate base for Casel's multifaceted model of mystery than the analogy which he drew with the rites of the pagan mystery religions. Thus, for example, in a paper read to the Adelaide Theological Circle, in Australia, on 31 October 1958, Gabriel brought together Casel's understanding of the Eucharist as the making present of the whole saving work of God in Christ, with a carefully argued exposition of the meaning of the Hebrew term, zikkaron, as found in Old Testament passages dealing with the Passover, (Exodus 12, and Deuteronomy 16), and rendered in English as 'remembrance', or 'memorial'; and on this basis spoke of the eucharistic action as a re-presentation and an actualisation of Christ's saving work. As the memorial of the Jewish Passover was a realisation of God's saving presence in the present time, so the memorial of the Eucharist was an actual realisation of the presence of Christ, 'a gathering, feeding, and sending of his people to be his Body in the world'. In this account of what, from a theological point of view, was happening in the eucharistic celebration, Gabriel is at pains to stress that it is a divine action, an action from eternity into time, and an action which is to be extended beyond the bounds of the physical church building, through the apostolic witness of the People of God; on this note he concludes by saying, 'It was from Maria Laach Abbey in Germany that I first learnt what I am persuaded is the true meaning of the words said at the end of mass: "Ite missa est"; not "Go, the mass is ended", but "Go, the church is dismissed" – dismissed from serving God in his temple to go out and serve him in his world. For this is the sphere of the proper work of the laity.'

It would not be an exaggeration to say that Gabriel's visit to the Continental centres of the Liturgical Movement in the summer of 1932, was one of the most significant episodes of his whole life. For on this occasion the contacts and conversations he had with the monks of Mont César and Maria Laach provided the inspiration for the greatest work of contributing to the renewal of the liturgical life of the Church of England, immediately prior to, and in a real sense of preparing the ground for, the era of liturgical revision and experimentation which began with the setting up of the Church of England's Liturgical Commission in 1955. His contact with the Liturgical Movement not only provided the main stream of inspiration for *Liturgy and Society,* but also enabled him to broaden and extend his ecumenical work, and enable the insights and convictions of that movement to challenge and enter into the thinking of other churches and traditions. A good example of this is the small ecumenical gathering which he arranged in the summer of 1933, on the general theme of Christian worship. The original idea for such a conference had come from Bishop Bell of Chichester, who had offered to accommodate the conference at the Bishop's Palace.

The conference took place from 18 to 24 of July, and was fully ecumenical, with Fr Bulkakoff and Dr Nicholas Zernov representing the Orthodox, a Swedish priest and German pastor representing the Lutherans, a Calvinist Reformed theologian, (in order as Gabriel said, 'to get the all important Barthian paper'), the Methodist scholar T.W.Manson, another British Free Church representative, and two Roman Catholics from the Continent. At this time, of course, Roman Catholics were officially prohibited from taking part in such ecumeni-

cal gatherings, but of the two who attended the Chichester conference, one was nominated by Mont César, and the other, Dom
Damasus Winzen was a monk of Maria Laach. In a draft programme,
headed 'confidential', which was circulated to all the British participants, Gabriel appended this important note, 'For the sake of the
Roman Catholics who are attending the conference it is highly
important that no notice of the meeting should appear in any
newspaper or journal; and also that none of us should mention it in
conversation'.

The conference was a success and a similar gathering was arranged
for 9 to 14 January 1936. The object of this second conference was to
examine some of the theological presuppositions of liturgical renewal,
and to discuss the wider social and ecumenical implications of such
renewal. Despite the shadow cast by political developments in Germany, the conference was another success. On his return to Maria
Laach, Damasus Winzen wrote to Gabriel to thank him for arranging
the conference and to say 'my trip to England was one of the best
things that have happened in my monastic career, above all on
account of the people who I met there'. The conference had been
fully ecumenical. The Congregationist scholar C. H. Dodd had taken
part, and so had the ecumenist J. H. Oldham. Bishop Bell had also
been personally involved, and his participation confirmed his own
view of the importance of the Liturgical Movement, and its capacity
to unlock the best resources for Christian life and worship. Shortly
after the conference Bell appointed a Diocesan Liturgical Missioner,
Henry de Candole, who some years later was to become a central
figure in the Parish and People Movement. Meanwhile, the political
situation in Germany was worsening, and Damasus Winzen's letters
to Gabriel became more anxious. In one of these letters, Damasus
tells of how the Nazis had introduced legislation prohibiting youth
groups and organisations from engaging in sports activities, which
curiously including walking and singing. This he claimed was a
tactical manoeuvre designed to make the Hitler Youth a more
attractive option for the young people of Germany. A consequence
of the legislation was that Maria Laach had to abandon its work
with young people. The situation was critical, and on February 1936,
Damasus wrote to Gabriel, saying, 'There can be no doubt that the
Government here wants to put an end to the Church and Christianity.
The monastery may close in the next few months. What can help is
countries like England, which respects freedom of opinion, bringing
some influence to bear on German politicians. . . . It is simply the

case that the English church can play an important role in mediation and reconciliation in the current situation in Germany, if it uses the opportunity well!'

The whole community began to feel that the situation was desperate. In 1938 they feared that the monastery would be supressed by the Nazis, and Damasus Winzen, and a small group of other German Benedictines, were sent to establish a safe house in the United States of America. Within a few months of negotiations, the monks opened a new house, St Paul's Priory in Utah. After the war the older monks returned to Germany, but Damasus remained and founded St Saviour's Monastery in New York.

Liturgy and Society

Gabriel's *Liturgy and Society* was generally well received and reviewed. A résumé of the book was given in the editorial of the July issue of the journal *Theology* in order to 'whet the appetite of readers'. One reviewer even suggested that Gabriel might fill the gap left by Gore, but some others were less flattering. The reviewer in the *New Statesman and Nation* reckoned that the illustrations in the book were horrible, and the Dominican friar, Aelwin Tindal-Atkinson, in *Blackfriars*, took Gabriel to task over his treatment of Thomism. Nevertheless, the book was an astonishing success. It went through five impressions in nine years, was translated into French, and in 1938, Gabriel wrote an introduction for a proposed Italian translation. The book itself was addressed to the general Christian reader and the intelligent enquirer who hovered on the threshold of the Church and wondered what the Christian life of faith might entail. Thus, Gabriel avoided using technical language and wrote in straightforward and lucid prose. One of the most significant achievement's of the book was the way in which it drew connections between a variety of sources and viewpoints. There was the thinking of Herwegen, Brilioth, Barth, and perhaps inevitably, F. D. Maurice, described by Gabriel as 'that seer and prophet of the future whose importance has never yet been fully recognised, and whose teaching will form the basis of the constructive theology of the future'. (*Lit. and Soc.* p.108). The book also commented on the work of church architects and artists, quoted the poetry of T. S. Eliot, whom Gabriel considered to be 'one of the most interesting figures in England today', and cited the work of the novelist D. H. Lawrence, who despite his avowed secular outlook, sometimes spoke, in

Gabriel's view, with a prophetic voice. From such a diverse range of writers and thinkers, Gabriel produced the kind of catholic work which was able to help the Church to articulate her self-understanding in the modern world.

The book itself began life as a series of articles which Gabriel wrote for the SSM Quarterly. The first, which appeared in the Christmas edition of 1932, was a description of the salient features of 'The Liturgical Movement in the Roman Catholic Church', and in response to a request engendered by this article, Gabriel wrote four others under the general title of 'The Liturgy in the Parish'. These articles offered some practical guidelines as to how the insights of the Continental Liturgical Movement might be applied in an English parochial setting. Through these articles, of course, Gabriel was introducing ideas which the majority of Roman Catholics in England were not to hear for another thirty years.

One of the stated aims of the book was to show 'how Christian dogma finds its typical expression in worship, and how Christian religion is not merely a way of piety for the individual soul, but is in the first place a participation in a common life'. Such a stated view conclusively demonstrates that Gabriel stood within the Maurician succession. It was F. D. Maurice, who having been drawn into a number of doctrinal disputes and controversies, came to hold the opinion that worship was the proper touchstone of theological reflection, and true guide of private prayer. As he testified in his biographical writings, 'The liturgy has been to me a great theological teacher, a perpetual testimony that the Father, the Son and the Spirit, the One God blessed for ever, is the author of all life, freedom, unity to men; that our prayers are nothing but responses to his voice speaking to us and in us'. (*Life* vol. 11, p. 359)

From the stated aim of wanting to show how Christian dogma finds its typical expression in the worship of the Church, we can confidently describe the book as a work of liturgical theology; a liturgical theology not in the sense of seeking to explicate the theological significance of given liturgical themes and motifs, but in seeing the gathered worshipping Church as being the first arena of theological apprehension and response. Worship, of course, is the activity of the gathered Church, and as such, a liturgical theology needs to be embedded in an ecclesiology, a conscious and logically ordered understanding of the Church as being, at one and the same time, both a divine and a human institution. Significantly then, the book is subtitled, 'The Function of the Church in the Modern

World'. Typically, Gabriel's view of the Church is not an abstract theoretical construction, but as an empirical sign of the Kingdom of Christ, (pace Maurice), contextualised in the social, political and cultural fabric of the human world. For this reason, he begins to tackle the question of the mission of the Church, of what the Church might have to offer the modern world, by seeking to establish a realistic estimate of the conditions of contemporary life. Effective mission, it seems, requires a conscious recognition of the real needs of the society it seeks to address. Gabriel's analysis of the modern world was Euro-centric and complex. In his reading of the current situation of society, Gabriel identified the following factors: the loss of a common, shared religious belief; the alienation experienced by those who felt themselves caught in the cogs of an industrial society; the depersonalising effect which resulted from being a part of large consortiums and large administrative organisations; the deceptive myth of material progress; the emergence of competing ideologies, particularly Fascism and Nazism; and the individualistic and privatising effect of liberalism. These were the major features and forces to be seen at work in the contemporary world, and the composite picture they presented was of a society in crisis, a society in a state of social and political flux. So, in his reading of the current situation, Gabriel saw European civilisation as being on the verge of disintegration. Europe was in crisis and required a humanising influence, and in his view, it was precisely at this point that the Church did have something vital to offer and bring to the modern world. For Christianity, as we have seen, was not regarded as a pious option for the private individual, but a participation in a common life, a life which alone could release the necessary power to remake a humane society and provide social cohesion and purpose. This conviction echoes the teaching of Beauduin and the other leaders of the twentieth-century Liturgical Movement, who passionately believed that by unlocking the inexhaustible resources of the Christian sacraments, the Church could become what she was called to be, the Body of Christ, given for the salvation of the world.

As the argument in *Liturgy and Society* unfolds, Gabriel's thinking crystalises to form three pivotal points. The first of these revolves around the relationship between worship and docrine. At this point he presupposes the principle of *lex orandi lex credendi*, the principle which states that the rule of faith, the substance of Christian belief is established by liturgical practice. Here again, Gabriel reveals his indebtedness to the thought of Maurice, in viewing Christian belief not as a closed doctrinal system, but as the formulation of the Chistian profession of faith, which both historically and logically finds its primary expression in the profession of personal allegiance to the triune God which is made in the context of worship. Closely related to this point of view is the conviction that the most immediate and potent force in the process of Christian formation, of a person becoming Christian, is the individual's participation in the Church's worship. Gabriel expresses the matter in these terms: 'By the influence of the Church service the regular Church people are moulded; for the things which they do in church makes a deeper impression than the teaching which reaches their minds.' (*Liturgy and Society*, p. 39, cf. p. 82 & 224). What is suggested here is that the very rudiments of Christian belief are built, as it were, into the very structures and forms of the Church's worship, and so a deeper entering into Christian worship can lead to a greater assimilation, both conscious and unconscious, of Christian truth. Thus a great deal of a person's knowledge of Christian faith is tacitly learnt, and so in this case, as in other areas of a person's life, it needs to be recognised that the individual knows a great deal more than he, or she, is able to articulate, or state in propositional form.

Nevertheless, although Christian truth cannot be precisely stated, or contained within an intellectual system of thought, it can and should be elucidated; here, at this point, Gabriel registers the strengths of 'Modernism', namely its demand for critical rigour, and its willingness to use the methods of historical investigation and face its results. (see *Lit. & Soc.* p. 34). So, Gabriel parts company with the Modernists not over their desire to test the compatibility of Christian truth-claims with other areas of human knowledge, but at the point where they reduce Christian dogma to the level of mere opinion. Gabriel asserts that Christian belief needs to be stated and stated authoritatively in a deliberately reasoned form. But again, the reader is reminded that Christian belief is first expressed in liturgical forms, and consequently, doctrinal statements always need to be seen as being secondary, derivative, and open to revision in the light of further knowledge and experience (see *Lit. & Soc.* pp. 113/4).

The second pivotal point in Gabriel's argument revolves around the relationship between Church and society. This point similarly evokes the teaching of the leaders of the continental Liturgical Movement, but in Gabriel's treatment of the issue, his starting point is characteristically biblical. He bases his account of the relationship between the Christian community and wider society on the Johannine paradox, which states that the Christian community is *in* the world, but not *of* the world. The origins and source of the Church's life are, as we might say today, transcendent and sacramentally mediated. For the Church is a human society divinely called, and constituted by Christ in the sacramental actions of Baptism and Eucharist, whose mission is to address and engage the social realities in which she is set. This, in Gabriel's view, is the substance to which the Johannine paradox points.

The central feature of the Church's life which shows her to be in contradistinction from the world, is her life as a praying community. Prayer is the essential activity of the Church. Furthermore, the Church which prays 'Thy kingdom come' is summoned to discern the divine purpose for the world, and to obey the divine will in actively revealing and promoting the Kingdom of Christ. But in this task, as Gabriel warns his readers, no single programme of social reform, or imagined utopia can be wholly identified with the cause of God. This assertion though, is not intended to mute the socially prophetic voice of the Church, but to underline the continuous necessity of a critical engagement of the Church in the social and political affairs of the world. With this qualification, the prophetic aspect of the Church's mission is presented with a singular clarity: 'The Church is called to protect and promote a proper humanism: the Church stands as the witness, against the world, of the right of a man to be treated as a human being'. (*Lit. and Soc.* p. 158)

Within Gabriel's perspective, prayer is seen as the proper spring-board of Christian action. The Christian, bound by his, or her, baptismal promise to reject evil and to follow Christ, is compelled to unmask evil and all that dehumanises and demeans people, and to dismantle its causes: 'Poverty, bad housing, the wrong distribution of wealth are material evils; and because they are evils, they must be fought against'. (*Lit. and Soc.* p. 202). Christians then, are called upon, when circumstances dictate, to raise the prophetic voice of the Church. They are to protest in the face of evil, and where the opportunity presents itself, to actively engage in practical loving service. All this springs from, and is sustained by prayer, for it is the Church's prayer, above all else, which is able to orientate the soul towards God, the ultimate Good and goal of human fulfilment, and being so orientated, the Christian is enabled to distinguish between good and evil, and actively engage in the kind of activity which is truly for the good of others. This is not to say that prayer is solely a means to an end, a means of making the Christian a more effective servant of God's kingdom; on the contrary, Gabriel is also wanting to assert the value of prayer in itself. The logic of Gabriel's argument unfolds like this: prayer should lead the Christian to action, but prayer too is a kind of action, and one which makes its own contribution to the healing of broken humanity. For as he says, '. . . be it remembered, in giving his social message, the prophet is not adding to the Christian Gospel something that was not there before. . . . we are to learn more and more to use the psalms, the kyrie eleison, the General Confession, not merely allying them to ourselves, but using them in order to share the common burden of the humanity of which we form a part. As Christians thus learn to exercise their priestly functions of intercession for the world, they will learn how to bring their practical contribution for the healing of its wounds'. (*Lit. and Soc.* p. 203)

For Gabriel, the praying Church is both the Christian's school for prophetic engagement, and the setting in which he, or she, can make a significant contribution to the task of making a more humane world. Furthermore, there is an important ecclesial dimension to this task of remaking human society in accord with the Kingdom. For the task of proclaiming the Kingdom is served as much by what the Church is called and empowered to be, as much as by the practical witness of her members. More specifically, it is what the Church is called and enabled to be as a eucharistic community which is of vital and intrinsic importance. One of Gabriel's favourite Patristic texts was a phrase from a sermon of Augustine of Hippo, in which he tells his hearers that they are to become what they receive, the Body of Christ. Now it is precisely as the Body of Christ, in which individuals are responsible to and for each other, that the Church can offer the world a model of what human society ought to be. For in drawing together people from every condition and background to be in communion with Christ, and in community with one another, the eucharistic community can be a humane and humanising community of persons, as Gabriel confidently asserts, 'In the midst of the levelling, disintegrating, and dehumanising influences of the modern social system, the Church even now creates a true social life'. The Church however, is not only a model of society, but also, through its sacramental celebrations, the theatre of societal renewal and transformation. For all that the Christian brings to the eucharistic assembly, as an individual and a member of the wider community, 'is re-orientated towards God as its centre, and is transformed, sanctified and glorified'. Here, Gabriel is not only alluding to the previously mentioned aspects of confession and intercession, but pointing to the human and divine action in the eucharistic celebration itself.

In an undated paper entitled 'The Meaning of Worship', but probably written in the late 1940s, Gabriel sets out a forceful critique of the view that the Church's task was to offer 'a devotional life' separate from, and disconnected to the public arena of daily life. It is, he argues, impossible to defend acts of worship without reference to their interpretative value in every field of human thought and action. The Eucharist especially, he says, cannot be fully understood without reference to its public and social significance. For the Eucharist is an effective demonstration of God's salvation and judgement, and the worshipping space is a theatre of human and divine activity, a place of encounter and transformation. For the bread and wine of the Eucharist, brought at the Offertory, and received as divine food and drink at Communion is 'drawn from the world of nature as that is exploited by manufacture and commerce. In the act of consecration judgement is passed upon the world in which bread and wine are cornered by speculators and adulterated by manufacturers; a world in which the interests of money actually misrepresent God's bounty and create an artificial poverty. The holy Eucharist takes the common means of bodily sustenance for which the sinful world struggles and swindles and restores them to their proper place as the instruments of human fellowship.' The social impact and implicature of the eucharistic action could not be more forcefully put than this rhetorical flourish of Gabriel Hebert.

The third point at which Gabriel's thinking crystallises in *Liturgy and Society* revolves around the relationship between worship and culture. This relationship is implicit throughout the book, and becomes explicit in the tantalisingly brief, but suggestive chapter entitled 'Christianity and Art'. Here again, Gabriel is inspired by, and quotes extensively from Abbot Herwegen of Maria Laach. Indeed, the very tone and tenor of Gabriel's argument in this chapter is summarised in these words from Herwegen's *Christliche Kunst und Mysterium*, which he cites at the beginning of the chapter, 'Christianity is in its essence not a doctrine but life, the life of Christ in the baptised. Wherever Christianity sheds its light, powerful impulses of life arise, which soon make themselves visible as creative or transforming forces in the outward world of phenomen. . . . the Christian conception of art worked a radical change, in contrast with the purely formal art of late antiquity, by assigning importance to the meaning (Inhalt) of artistic work. . . . In all the life expression of the Christian, and therefore also in his art, there is seen the utterance of 'the Word' in the double sense of the Christian idea, and of its relation to the Divine Word, the Logos'.

The abbey of Maria Laach actively promoted Christian art, offering studio facilities to artists, and three examples of work from Maria Laach provided some of the illustrations in *Liturgy and Society*. These three pieces of sculpture, 'The Word made flesh', 'Immaculata', and 'Our Lady of the Lily', are in themselves unexceptional as pieces of art, but show the simple line and clarity which has been associated with the functionalist art which was in vogue in the 1930s. In his discussion of Christian art, Gabriel does not take the reader very far beyond the thinking of Herwegen. In presenting Herwegen's line of thought, Gabriel argues that with the developments in Renaissance art, especially its 'realism' and its psychological interest in its subjects, something of the imaginative potency of religious art had been lost. At this point, Gabriel invokes the Eastern Orthodox tradition of icon painting, and from this basis, draws the conclusion that authentic Christian art should be free from all superfluous and distracting decoration, and should, like the Eastern icon, disclose and show the transcendent meaning of its subject.

Apart from these comments on art, Gabriel draws the reader's attention to the question of church architecture, but here his comments are largely concerned with style, and the requirement that church architects should be faithful to the traditions of ecclesiastical architecture and sensitive to the contemporary needs of the worshipping community. To be concerned with one, at the expense of the other, can only result in a building which is inadequate as the setting for Christian worship. At this point in Gabriel's discussion, he is underlining the importance of the ambience of worship. The liturgy, he claimed, required a proper setting, because its meaning was expressed as much in its outward performance, as in the meaning of the liturgical texts which were used. Furthermore, the physical setting of the liturgy had to be such as to facilitate the participation of the whole assembly in the sacred drama, for 'liturgical forms, like drama, are composed to be acted; and again, they differ from drama in that there is no audience, and all those present share in the action'. (*Lit. and Soc.* p. 246). Following this line of argument, it would not be an exaggeration to describe worship as an art-form, and church services as being liturgical performances. Such vocabulary need not necessarily imply that worship should be an aesthetic experience, but it certainly reminds us that liturgy is a deliberately shaped composition, consisting of texts to be said, or sung, music, movement, costume, visual images, symbols and sacramental signs. What Gabriel has to say about the nature of symbols, at this point, is interesting and informative. When he speaks of symbols in a liturgical context, he is not using the term symbol in the way in which the term might be used in everyday conversation, when it might be used in saying that something was a 'mere symbol'. Liturgical symbols, he asserts, are not simply signs, or illustrations of something else, but themselves actually evoke, express and convey the reality which they symbolise. This view of symbols, and symbolic actions, is expressed in the following terms:

> 'A God whom our limited minds could demonstrate and comprehend would thereby be proved not to be the true God. Because his ways are not our ways, nor his thoughts our thoughts, our thoughts of him must work with symbols, images and rituals; it is through a glass darkly that we now see. But we can believe that there are symbols and images of truth and rituals having contact with reality, because they are subject to and controlled by the fact of the coming of God in the flesh, in history'. (*Lit. and Soc.* p. 250).

The performance of Christian worship, like authentic Christian art, it seems, ought to express and evoke the object of worship, the divine reality of the triune God, whose own art is the refashioning of creation.

Doing the Liturgy

Liturgical renewal was precipitated by the virtual blocking of liturgical revision in 1928, and the scope of this renewal is well indicated by the pivotal points of Gabriel's thinking in *Liturgy and Society*, which has been discussed above. Without the immediate prospect of the revision of liturgical texts in the Church of England, it was inevitable that attention should be drawn to the practical arrangements of liturgical life in parishes, its setting and mode of celebration, and again in this regard Gabriel's writing was influential. The kind of changes in the practice of liturgy outlined by Gabriel, might well be viewed as the legacy of the Liturgical Movement, and typically include: (1) the re-introduction of the offertory; (2) westward celebration; (3) concelebration; and (4) regular communion, changes which now are long established, and require a critical evaluation.

1 The Offertory rite

We have seen that the watchword of the continental Liturgical Movement was participation, and that its major aim was to promote the active participation of the faithful in the worship of the Church. The proponents of the Movement firmly believed that the offertory rite in the mass provided a supreme opportunity for the participation of the faithful in the bringing up of the bread and wine for the eucharistic sacrifice. This renewed interest in the offertory was seized upon by Gabriel and enthusiastically described in *Liturgy and Society*. In this description of the offertory, it is transparent that he considered the offertory procession to have been common practice in the early Church: 'The offertory in these early days must have been a very impressive act. The communicants brought their oblations of bread and wine (and sometimes other gifts too) and presented them at the altar'. (*Lit. and Soc.* p. 76)

The claim that Gabriel makes here is undoubtedly exaggerated. In the early centuries of the Christian Church the faithful probably did bring gifts of bread and wine for use at the Eucharist, but there is no early historical evidence for offertory processions as we would understand them. Those who brought gifts, (and in North Africa at the time of Augustine, this seems to have been the pious practice of well-heeled women), probably left them in a room set apart for the purpose. At some point in the celebration, and we do not really know exactly at what point, how, or by whom, the bread and the wine required for the Eucharist would be brought to the bishop at the altar.

In the 1960s and 1970s, when liturgical revision was proceeding at fever pitch the offertory rite received particular attention. At this time it was argued that the proliferation of offertory prayers, (the *Oratio super oblata* of the old Roman rite), rather confused the issue by anticipating in their vocabulary the aspect of sacrifice, which strictly speaking belongs in the eucharistic prayer, and comes after the Institution narrative and anamnesis, ('Remembering his death, resurrection . . .' etc.). After Vatican II, the revisers changed the nomenclature from 'offertory' to 'presentation', or 'preparation of the gifts' in order to clarify the proper character of the offertory rite. The compilers of the Church of England's *The Alternative Service*

Book (*1980*) were equally precise, and the rubical directions in the Rite A Communion service indicate that the 'Preparation of the Gifts' is to be regarded as a practical preliminary for the thanking, or blessing.

Gabriel, of course, had accepted the historical assumptions of the leaders of the Liturgical Movement, but the importance he attached to physical movement and active participation in the liturgy was sound. He was correct, for instance, in claiming that liturgy was primarily an action. In all aspects of human behaviour, including the use of language, the act is primitive, and a good case could be constructed to argue that symbolic action and gesture is the real grammar of worship. As Gabriel himself argued in a paper read to an ecumenical group of Anglican and Roman Catholic theologicans 'Liturgy needs to be regarded concretely; the printed texts are related to Liturgy itself much as the printed score of a symphony is related to the symphony itself, performed by an orchestra and listened to by an intelligent and co-operative audience. Similarly liturgy is properly an action, *here* and *now*, of *this* local unit of the Church assembled for the worship of God.' From the perspective shown here, the real challenge to the liturgist today, equipped with a wide repertoire of liturgical texts, is to devise and suggest the kind of practical arrangements and ceremonial which might function as a kind of counterpoint to the action of God in sacramental worship.

The Orthodox liturgist and lay theologian, W. Jardine Grisbrooke, once made the interesting comment that the offertory procession as generally practised in parish churches, with members of the congregation bringing up the gifts of bread and wine to the altar in procession from a table at the back of the church was a token and rather theatrical gesture.[8] The point is a valid one. Good litugy is dramatic, but the discerning liturgist needs to distinguish between the dramatic and the theatrical, that is, between the kind of action which strikes and engages the attention of others, and that which is contrived. One way of avoiding the theatricality of the offertory, suggested by Grisbrooke, is to make the offertory more substantial, with the presentation of bread which has been baked and brought from the home. On this basis, together with Gabriel's view that the celebration of the Christian mysteries involves a material and spiritual transaction, a carefully and imaginatively planned offertory rite might well be justified.

2 *Westward Celebration*

The move towards the restoration of westward celebration, of the president facing the people during the eucharistic prayer, was largely

motivated by a utilitarian reason. This reason, clearly stated by
Gabriel in *Liturgy and Society* was to arrange the celebration in such
a way as to facilitate a greater participation on the part of the
congregation. It was understood that the Eucharist was the celebration of the whole assembly, and not solely that of the officiating
priest. So, as Gabriel explains, in a few places on the continent, the
position of the altar has been changed so that 'the priest could stand
on the far side of it facing the people, with the object of bringing the
people more in touch with the liturgical action.' (*Lit. and Soc.* p. 129).
This re-positioning of the altar invariably involved bringing the altar
forward from the east wall of the sanctuary, or the setting up of a
nave altar. Such an arrangement for westward celebration has now
become commonplace. The use of a nave altar serves a double
function; it not only helps people to see the priest's actions during
the eucharistic prayer and the fraction, but also renders more clearly
the meal aspect of the Eucharist, with the people of God gathered
around the Lord's table. This latter symbolic meaning is not, of
course, without precedent in the history of Anglican liturgy. The
rubical instructions concerning the use of a table in the chancel,
which are found in the Communion Office of the 1552 English
Prayer Book, clearly indicates Cranmer's desire to emphasise the
meal aspect of the Holy Communion. The critical point which needs
to be made, however, arises from the view that the Eucharist is a
multi-faceted mystery, and consists in the fact that different arrangements for celebrating the liturgy might highlight different aspects of
that mystery. An eastward celebration, for instance, which evokes
the primitive Christian eschatological expectation of the coming of
the Lord, might well be an appropriate arrangement to use in the
Sundays in Advent, the traditional season of the Christian year when
the Church prepares herself to welcome and receive her coming
Lord. There is, after all, a patent need in the performance of the
Church's liturgy to signal both the transcendence of God, his essential
Otherness, as well as his imminence. This second aspect of 'the
transcendent in our midst', can certainly be effectively expressed in a
sensitively performed westward celebration, but this should not
preclude the occasional eastward celebration, particularly in those
church buildings designed for that mode of celebration. Perhaps in
the final analysis, clergy and all those involved in the planning of
liturgy, should not allow themselves to become too fixed on any one
style, or mode of celebration. The important concern is to allow the
liturgy to have its full and proper dramatic impact, always conscious

of the fact that the real actor in the saving drama enacted in the Eucharist is the triune God, Father, Son, and Holy Spirit.

3 Concelebration

The question of eucharistic concelebration was introduced to English readers through Gabriel's article on the subject published in *Theology*, in February, 1931. The basis of this article was a discussion of concelebration which had been written by Lambert Beauduin, and published in *Les Questions Liturgiques et Paroissiales*, in 1922. The practice of concelebration was again cited by Gabriel in *Liturgy and Society*, as a model of communal celebration. Gabriel evidently considered concelebration as an example of the essentially corporate and participative character of the liturgy in the early church; a liturgical celebration in which the various ministers performed particular roles, according to their order. According to this rather homogeneous picture of the liturgy of the early church:

> 'The Bishop was when possible the celebrant, and was surrounded by his priests, who (at least at Rome) concelebrated with him; the deacons, headed by the archdeacon, and the subdeacons had their share in the reading of the lessons and the ceremonial of the altar: chanters and choir, acolytes and doorkeepers all had their place; the people too had their share in the action, in the offering of the gifts and the kiss of peace and the communion'. (*Lit. and Soc.* p. 75)

It is undoubtedly the case that some form of concelebration was practised in the early Church and persisted in the West into the Middle Ages, but exactly how it was arranged, and whether it was a universal practice is open to dispute. What can be said, is that concelebration continued in the West on particular occasions, such as ordinations, but its survival is really seen in the Eastern Byzantine rite. Beauduin's interest in concelebration was undoubtedly fired by his interest in the Byzantine rite, and his desire to foster a greater mutual understanding between Roman and Byzantine Christians. Concelebration would also have appealed to Beauduin as a mode of celebration which could replace the practice of private masses. In his view, the private mass, offered by a priest with the assistance of a server, was responsible for the inculcation of the excessive individualism in eucharistic piety, which he was seeking to correct.

Gabriel in his writing was not particularly concerned to restore the practice of sacerdotal concelebration, but to marshal further evidence to support his central contention that the Eucharist ought to be a corporate offering the work of the whole eucharistic assembly.

The renewed interest in concelebration, stimulated by Beauduin and other Roman Catholics on the continent, inevitably led to questions as to how exactly concelebration ought to be arranged. The Eastern model of 'ceremonial concelebration', of other ministers being vested in the sanctuary, according to their order, did not satisfy those priests who were anxious to know whether a concelebrating priest could be said to have 'offered the holy sacrifice'. A practical and important corollary of this question, was the issue of whether a concelebrating priest was qualified to receive a mass stipend. A definitive answer to these questions was eventually given by Pope Pius XII, at the Assisi Pastoral Liturgical Congress, on 22 September 1956. On that occasion the Pope declared that in the case of concelebration, 'Christ acts not through one minister, but through several', (c.f. Thomas Aquinas, S.T. III Q82, art. 2), and ruled that 'It is enough for the concelebrants to have and to manifest the intention of making their own the words and actions of the celebrant; they themselves say the words "This is my body", "This is my blood", or their concelebration will be limited to the realm of external ceremonial'. This statement contained the basis for an understanding of 'sacramental concelebration', which was to be refined in the various degrees and regulations which were to follow in the wake of the Second Vatican Council. The end, and unsatisfactory, result is that concelebration became too narrowly defined in terms of co-consecration, and consequently, concelebrated Eucharists are choreographed in such a way as to make concelebration look and sound like a huddled clerical con-mumble. Alternatively, when the various parts of the eucharistic prayer are distributed among the concelebrants, another problem arises, namely a confusion of the role of the liturgical president; a role which has been emphasised in recent liturgical revision, and which requires to be clearly focused in one person.

It is unfortunate that some Catholic-minded Anglicans have so readily and uncritically adopted the Roman practice of concelebration. Some Anglo-Catholics defend their practice in terms drawn from *Sacrosactum Concilium*, (1965), which speaks of concelebration as being a way of showing the 'unity of the priesthood' but this is a spurious concept, and one which trades at the expense of the unity of the whole eucharistic assembly. The Eucharist should never be over-clericalised to such a degree that it unbalances the unity of the assembly for the Eucharist itself is pre-eminently the sacrament of unity, and should be celebrated in such a way as to manifest the unity of the gathered priestly people of God, both ordained and lay.

4 Regular Communion

The question of encouraging the practice of regular Communion was taken up in Gabriel's promotion of the Parish Communion, 'a parallel development to the Liturgical Movement in the Roman Catholic Church', (Lit. and Soc. p. 213). We know from a talk which he gave to a group of Swedish clergy in the summer of 1928, that he favoured the Parish Communion, that is, a Eucharist with Commun-ion of the people as the chief and central act of parochial Sunday worship. The Parish Communion had been established in the early 1920s in the rural parish of Temple Balsall, in Warwickshire, and in the urban parish of St John's, Newcastle. In both places a full sung Eucharist had been established at 9 am, and judging by the level of attendance, the service was meeting a pastoral need. In Gabriel's mind, the great blunder of the Anglo-Catholic Movement was its dogged continuance of a non-communicating High Mass, at 11.00 am, and its slowness in adopting the Parish Communion:

> 'If the Anglo-Catholic Movement after the war had been far seeing enough to return to the practice of the early church and adopt the Parish Eucharist with Communion as the principal service of the Sunday, the whole situation of the Church of England would now be different; and the Parish Eucharist would have universally justified itself as truly evangelical and truly catholic'. (Lit. and Soc p. 211)

Apart from the reluctant Anglo-Catholics, there were others, in this case of a liberal persuasion, who failed to share Gabriel's enthusiasm for the cause. Soon after the publication of Liturgy and Society, the editor of the journal, Modern Churchman, in refering to the book in his editorial article, ventured the opinion that the arrangement of a Parish Communion was not only undesirable, but also impracticable.[9]

However, experiments in various parishes were proving to be successful, and the expectation that the people were going to play a part in the celebration of the Church's liturgy was growing, and on

this latter front, Kelham was making a small, but significant contribution. George Every, in his unpublished autobiographical writings,
has drawn attention to the fact that in the 1920s and 1930s, students
being ordained from Kelham would have found the general pattern
of Sunday services in parishes quite unsatisfactory. At Kelham they
had become accustomed to a full participatory and sung Eucharist at
8.30 am, on Sundays. Inadvertedly, the Sunday liturgical arrangements which had developed quite accidently at Kelham, would have
raised in the minds of its theological students the expectation of an
early Sunday morning sung Communion. The usual pattern of Sunday
morning worship found by ordinands in their title parishes would
have been an early morning said celebration of Communion, with
the main service at 11.00 am. In most churches this service would
have been Choral Mattins. By the mid-1930s, there were a number of
parishes who were willing to experiment, and what they needed was
some practical advice and guiding wisdom as to how best to implement the change.

In 1935, a restless and self-styled 'Liturgical Missioner', Edward
Bulstrode, (Br Edward), who had been based at Temple Balsall in the
1920s, wrote to Gabriel after a sleepless night, suggesting that he
might write a book on the Parish Eucharist, a book which would
bring together the best experience of those priests who had success-
fully implemented the Parish Communion in their parishes. The
result was the publication of *The Parish Communion* (SPCK, 1937).
This book was a collection of some fourteen essays, some practically
based, and others more theoretical. The contributors included a
brilliant Anglican theologian, Austin Farrer, who wrote an essay on
the Eucharist and the Church in the New Testament, Henry de
Candole, and Dom Gregory Dix. Dix's 'fat green book', *The Shape
of the Liturgy* (Dacre, 1945), a book which had a colossal influence
on the shape of liturgical revision in the late 1950s and 1960's, was in
fact an expanded version of his essay in *The Parish Communion*.
Together with these more theological essays, were essays by parish
priests, from country, town, and city parishes, offering insights from
their own experience of implementing the Parish Communion. In the
first nine months the book sold some 2,500 copies, proof in itself that
the book was meeting a recognised pastoral and liturgical need.
Trevor Beeson has claimed that 'few, if any collections of essays have
had such a dramatic effect on the life of a church'.[10]

Although Gabriel was prompted by Br Edward into editing a book
on the Parish Communion, he certainly had his own conception of

what such a book ought to achieve, and his aim was explicitly stated in the letter he wrote to Gregory Dix at Nashdom, soliciting a contribution from him. In this letter, Gabriel said, 'This book must altogether avoid the danger of treating the parish mass as a stunt. It has got to go into the principle of the thing, and it has got to be in effect a book of the Liturgical Movement in the Church of England.' This declared aim is incontrovertible evidence that Gabriel's espousal and advocacy of the Parish Communion was the result of what he had learnt from the Continental Liturgical Movement. Thus, in his own essay in *The Parish Communion* he says, 'The movement for the establishing of the Parish Communion must not be side-tracked by being made into some sort of ritualistic movement. It is, in fact, part of the Liturgical Movement which is going on in our day in every part of Christendom, and which is fundamentally a movement of return to the sacraments and the liturgy, as the sacramental expression of our redemption through Christ and of the nature of the Church as his mystical Body'.

In the Preface to the book, Gabriel explains that his concern was not simply to promote a particular arrangement for parish Sunday worship, but to let the conception of the Church as the people of God dictate the form and type of the main Sunday service. Accordingly, his first stated objective is to 'set forth a conception of the nature of the Church, which appears to compel the adoption of the Parish Communion as its necessary expression in liturgy. It is the idea of the Church that is primary'. (*The Parish Communion*, p.vii). In other words, the theological rationale for the Parish Communion was ecclesiological, a particular conception of the Church as the mystical Body of Christ, a conception, which in turn, was suggested and generated by the Church's celebration of the Eucharist. For as he argued, two years earlier in *Liturgy and Society*, the understanding of the Church as the mystical Body of Christ was most clearly shown and apprehended 'with the recovery of the true place of the Holy Eucharist in the life of the Church.' (*Lit. and Soc.* p.13). Thus, in Gabriel's mind, his understanding of the nature of the Church, and his understanding of the Eucharist are held in the closest tension, so that the one illuminates and informs the other, and produces what can best be described as a eucharistic ecclesiology, an understanding of the Church as manifested in the eucharistic assembly.

Although the various contributors to *The Parish Communion* were broadly from the Catholic wing of the Church of England, it was hoped that the book would have a more general appeal. Clearly both

Evangelicals and Anglo-Catholics would have to make considerable adjustments in their thinking and practice if they were to implement the Parish Communion in their parishes. However, the internal matters of the Church of England were soon to be overtaken by other events, particularly the worsening political situation in Europe and the eventual outbreak of war.

After the Second World War a new impetus towards liturgical renewal was launched with the inauguration of 'Parish and People', a loosely linked organisation which came to be seen as the 'Parish Communion Movement'. 'Parish and People' began with a small and select conference which was held at the Queen's College, Birmingham in 1949. At that conference Gabriel was appointed to serve on the Council of Parish and People, but at that stage, he realised that the future of the movement really lay in the hands of its younger members. Gabriel was then sixty-three, and for some time he had been absorbed in the field of biblical studies. At the first open conference arranged by 'Parish and People' Gabriel was invited to address the conference on the question of the relationship between liturgy and biblical theology, an issue which, as we shall see in the following chapter, was one which had exercised his mind for some time. At this time, Gabriel also renewed his contacts with the continental Liturgical Movement and actively sought to keep himself informed of developments on the continent. One of the most significant developments there, was the work of the Centre de Pastoral Liturgique, which had been established in Paris in 1940, and immediately after the war became an important centre for conferences and publications. Its journal, *La Maison Dieu*, disseminated the views of a galaxy of liturgists and liturgical theologians, and by comparison, made the English 'Parish and People' magazine seem lightweight and popular. Gabriel attended a conference at the Centre de Pastoral Liturgique in the autumn of 1950, and on that occasion heard accounts of developments in the thinking of the Liturgical Movement, and learnt of the switch of interest from the mass to the sacraments of Christian initiation, and the baptismal basis of Christian life. A colourful account of this conference, and of the various liturgical celebrations which he attended during his visit to Paris, was printed in the *Church Times*, on 3 November 1950.

Throughout the 1950s, when Gabriel was in Australia, the Parish Communion grew in popularity, and this was due in no small measure to the efforts of the 'Parish and People' movement. The whole period, of course, was a period of optimism and innovation, in both Church and state. The Church of England was in a confident mood, and the setting up of a Liturgical Commission in 1955 reopened the whole business of liturgical revision. In 1956, Michael Ramsey, then Bishop of Durham, published a short, but pithy critique of the Parish Communion.[11] In this article he set out his assessment of the strengths and weaknesses of the Parish Communion. The service, he claimed, had been an immense gain in making the Eucharist the centre of Sunday worship. He rejoiced in the fact that the service had been adopted in parishes across the spectrum of churchmanship, and the ways in which it had helped congregations to realise that they were the Church, the people of God, called into a common life as the Body of Christ. But alongside this positive estimate of the effects of the Parish Communion, Ramsey also identified three weaknesses, or possible dangers. The first was his concern that with the establishing of the Parish Communion, it was all too easy for individuals to equate worship with receiving Communion, and his comments in this regard point to what a more recent commentator, the theologian John Macquarrie, has called the problem of 'indiscriminate communions'.

Ramsey's second reservation concerned the way in which the proponents of the Parish Communion emphasised the term 'fellowship'. This term, he felt, was being overplayed to such an extent, that it was inviting misunderstanding. So, he drew attention to the fact that the meaning of the term in the New Testament, referred to the Christian's participation in the life of the crucified and risen Christ, and not to any experience of 'fellow-feeling', or 'bonhomie'. The danger Ramsey saw was that the Parish Communion might come to be seen as an exclusive gathering, the service for the truly committed Christian, and one at which the more tentative Christian, and the enquirer might feel uncomfortable.

Ramsey's most trenchant criticism, and one which apparently he never repented of, concerned the undue emphasis which some proponents of the Parish Communion were placing upon the offertory. The new movement places much emphasis upon the offertory, he said, and alluding to a mining parish in his own diocese of Durham, related how 'layfolk carry the elements in procession from the back of the church, and lumps of coal and other objects' as tokens of the offering to God of ordinary people's ordinary lives. In all this, Ramsey caught a whiff of Pelagianism, and detected a muddling of the doctrine of sacrifice. So, in unequivocal terms, he declared that 'we cannot, and we dare not, offer anything of our own apart from the one sacrifice of the Lamb of God'. On this question of sacrifice and the celebration of the Eucharist, it could be argued that the most eloquent and suitably placed gesture of offering comes during the doxology of the thanksgiving prayer, when the celebrant raises the chalice and the ciborium. This gesture, if it is performed in a generous and expressive way, can signal to the gathered assembly that through the rehearsal of God's saving drama, we ourselves are caught up with Christ's offering of himself in love and obedience to the Father; and only after that point in the liturgical celebration, and in communion with Christ, can the Christian pray 'we offer you our souls and bodies to be a living sacrifice'.

Today, the problems and opportunities for providing the kind of parochial liturgical life to inspire and nourish the people of God, are different to what they were thirty or forty years ago. After a period of well over twenty-five years of liturgical revision and experimental services, attempting to forge a liturgy which is appropriately shaped and expressed in contemporary language, perhaps we now need to turn our attention from questions of texts and language, and address what has been appropriately described as the 'crisis of symbolism', and seek to regain a greater appreciation of the essentially symbolic and ritual elements in liturgical celebrations.

Further problems and opportunities are presented by the fact that recent years have seen an increasing interest in so-called 'family services', and this, together with other factors, has caused a shift away from eucharistic worship. Behind this trend has been the important and legitimate concern with the part that children can and should play in the worship of the Church; but perhaps we might also cite as another contributory cause the political climate of the past decade, with its questioning of the very notion of 'society', and the emergence of the nuclear family as the focus of social and economic life in the west. These, and many other factors, such as the need for more immediate religious experience, as evidenced by the charismatic movement, have conspired to call in question the suitability of the Parish Communion as being the chief and central service of parochial Sunday worship. However, the central question which needs to be faced is whether the Parish Communion should be supplanted by non-sacramental worship? The answer to this question from the witness of the New Testament, and the weight of liturgical tradition seems to be unequivocal. According to Paul, in 1 Corinthians, ch.11, the Lord's Supper is the distinctive source and pattern of Christian worship. It is the occasion when Christians gather in joyful obedience to 'Do this in memory of me', and thereby are constituted as church, as the assembled people of God, to be the Body of Christ in the contemporary world. Thus we are constrained to see that the real challenge to the liturgist, and all who are involved in the planning and leading of the Church's worship, is to devise ways of supplementing, rather than supplanting eucharistic worship, in the liturgical and catechetical life of the Church.

Historically speaking, we might also note that the success of the Parish Communion contained the very seeds of its failure; for the very fact that it was so rapidly established in the 1950's, might mean that the theological principles and convictions which first undergirded its implementation by an earlier generation, were soon forgotten. Perhaps the time is long overdue for the Church to awaken from her amnesia in this respect, and rediscover, and possibly develop further, the theological, liturgical and ecclesial insights which gave the original direction and depth to the practice of the Parish Communion.

5
THE BIBLE AND WORSHIP

THE GREATEST part of Gabriel's long working life as a teacher and a writer, in England and Australia, was taken up with biblical studies. At Kelham his first Lecture Scheme on the four Gospels was printed in 1927, and these were radically rewritten in 1941, and a new set of lectures on the epistle to the Hebrews being written in 1942. One of his students, Fr Peter Clark SSM, once remarked that his notes were good, but as a lecturer he was awful. The written word was obviously his medium. He was a prolific writer, but wrote piecemeal and would solicit and welcome responses to what he had written. In this way, his books gradually evolved. He was not a biblical specialist in the technical sense of the word, but he worked with a scholarly attention to detail, and the writing itself was always clearly expressed and readable. In Gabriel's view, biblical scholars had invariably paid an inordinate attention to questions regarding the text and its background and had failed to draw the theological meaning from the texts themselves. It was precisely this latter task which exercised his mind and excited his interest. He was concerned to elicit and expound the theological significance of the Bible, and to communicate this to the theological student, the parish priest, the preacher, and the intelligent and enquiring Christian.

A task which particularly intrigued him was the task to discern and describe from a Christian perspective the relationship between the Old and New Testament, the Hebrew and Christian scriptures contained and conveyed by the biblical canon. This provided a constant theme running through all his books on the Bible. In the 1930s Gabriel had wanted to break the silence of the Old Testament in the Church, and argued for the restoration of an Old Testament reading in the Sunday eucharistic lectionary. This, of course, had been lost for a millennium in the western Church. In this respect his hopes were realised, for the Old Testament has found a place in the Ministry of the Word in the eucharistic services of the major traditions, both Catholic and Protestant, since the mid-1960s. Twenty-five years on, when Lectionary revision has returned to the agenda, the question of how the Hebrew Scriptures are to be viewed and used in the context of Christian worship is very much a live issue. Within this discussion one of the pressing questions is how to broaden the basis on which the Old Testament reading on a given Sunday relates to the New Testament readings. In the Roman Lectionary of 1969, the Old Testament reading was chosen to illustrate the Gospel, by setting the context, or by marking a contrast. But the question has been raised as to whether the Old Testament is always a help to understanding the Gospel passage.[1] The lectionary produced by the ecumenical Joint Liturgical Group, adopted for the Church of England's *The Alternative Service Book 1980*, allowed the three readings to be thematically controlled, but again the thematic linkage is not always obvious. Behind the particular discussion on Lectionary revision is the more radical question of how, and in what ways the two testaments are linked, and it is this question which Gabriel's biblical writings might help the reader to reach a deeper understanding.

The Old and New Testaments

In Gabriel's view, there were vast tracts of Old Testament writing which seemed to point beyond themselves, were essentially incomplete and demanded some future fulfilment. His first major book on the Bible *The Throne of David* (Faber, 1941) is significantly subtitled A Study of the Fulfilment of the Old Testament. The term 'fulfilment' is notoriously ambiguous. At one level it might signal a line of continuity, or as one recent writer has put it, 'a renewal and restoration of the original intention'.[2] This we might describe as the weak sense of the term. A strong sense of the term would indicate that the original, and intended meaning of the text was in some sense enlarged, literally filled-full, by the occurrence of some subsequent event, or appearance of some other figure. Undoubtedly for Gabriel, whatever might be meant by the expression 'fulfilment of scripture' had to be centred upon Jesus Christ, crucified and risen. But this is not to say that the Hebrew Scriptures were full of Messianic predictions. On the contrary, the New Testament did not render the Old Testament obsolete, and although it can be read through Christian eyes, the Christian must not expect to see Christ everywhere. The Old Testament was not to be subordinated to a Christian reading, but must be allowed to speak for itself as Scripture, and this view was clearly safeguarded by Gabriel in those places where he spoke of the 'positive meanings' of the Old Testament.

Thus he recognised the integrity of the individual books of the Old Testament, and, by implication, suggested that the Old Testament was able to convey to the reader an authentic knowledge of God. The historic Israel did know God, and in suggesting that her writings prior to Christ's historic coming were incomplete, was to say that in some sense it was Christ who answered their quest. The light of the Old Testament, to put it another way, is not eclipsed by the coming of Jesus, but serves to illuminate the significance of his coming. Textually speaking, the point is demonstrated by the fact that the Old Testament imagery and categories of law, wisdom, innocent suffering and divine kinship, directly contributed to the primitive church's understanding of Jesus' mission and fate, and to some extent provided the vocabulary with which he could proclaim his own message of the dawning of God's Kingdom. With this understanding, it is easy to appreciate why the Old Testament is indispensable for a correct reading of the New Testament.

Gabriel was writing at a time when anti-Semiticism was rife and at its cruellist in Nazi Germany. To his credit, Gabriel reminded his Christian readers of their indebtedness to the Hebrew Scriptures, and for his appeal for a greater sympathy and greater sense of continuity of faith in the one God, whom Christians claim to be the Father of Jesus Christ.

His attempt to present the Old Testament as an indispensable subject for serious Christian reflection was mounted on the one hand in opposition to the limited and literalistic reading of the fundamentalists, and on the other hand, against the liberal commentators of his own day who tended to disregard the Old Testament in their treatment of the New. Gabriel's aims, first sketched out in *The Throne of David* received a more substantial and systematic treatment in *The Authority of the Old Testament* (Faber, 1947). This book opens with an accusation that modern Christian theologians had generally failed to seriously engage the Old Testament in a theological way, and that conservatives had failed to meet the constructive challenges of historical criticism. For Gabriel historical criticism was inescapable for a religion which was so closely bound up with particular historical events and characters. The serious student of the Bible should not evade the uncertainties produced by the results of historical criticism, and Gabriel encourages the reader to be 'sharply and even daringly critical'. He saw, however, that this critical approach needed to be matched with an equally important appreciation that God can, and does, communicate to us through the reading and hearing of scripture. So Gabriel insists that the reader should be rigorously critical and at the same time 'deeply sensitive to the things of the Spirit'. The Bible had to engage the mind, and also, the imagination. For as he wrote in an article, 'The Bible in the Church', the Bible presents to the reader 'not so much theological formulae and precise definitions, but rather imagery on which the mind can dwell and on which the imagination can fix', and he believed that through the imagination something of God could be apprehended and understood. It is the living imagery of scripture, he asserts in this article, which gives the reader 'the substance of the faith, its flesh and blood'.[3]

Undoubtedly there is a wide body of literature which can sustain and nourish Christian faith, but the Bible holds a privileged position because of its canonical status. The word 'canon' was a relatively late addition to the Christian's vocabulary, and literally meant a standard, or rule, and was used to settle the question as to which texts were to be included, or to be more precise, to decide which texts were to be excluded from the Christian Bible. The question of the canon of Christian scripture was not finally settled until the fourth century, but it is first invoked in the second century Muratorian fragment, which indicates that the intention of the canon was to guard the earliest witness to the content of Christian faith. The criterion for recognition was apostolic authorship, or association, but significantly, the canon is presented as a list of books to be read in Church, to be read to the assembled people of God. In this sense, it could be argued that the canon was, at least in part, determined by the needs of the worshipping community.

Unsurprisingly, Gabriel exploits the fact that the canon was shaped by the worshipping traditions of the Jewish Synagogue and Christian assembly, and argues in the final chapter of *Authority*, that scripture and tradition are inextricably bound up together. Furthermore, the authority which is ascribed to scripture is closely related to its canonical status as a liturgical book. Again the difficult question of the inspiration of scripture is closely related to the question of the canon. Gabriel rejected the conservative view which regarded the individual writers and compilers of the biblical books as being themselves inspired, and dismissed as being unhelpful the liberal view that there were different degrees of inspiration within the Bible as a whole. What he proposed was that inspiration was a function of the canon itself, and acknowledged that 'In thus refusing to identify inspiration with the personal insight of each writer, and attributing it to the canon as a whole, we are laying a great weight on the canon, and asserting a providential guidance in the formation of the canon'. (*Authority*, p. 106)

The Church's canon of scripture has bound together both Hebrew and Christian texts, and the very fact that these books are accorded canonical status posits particular constraints and strategies for reading these texts, and one of these strategies, suggested by the very origins of the canonical process, is the use of the Bible within a liturgical context. It is as if the continuous liturgical use of the Bible keeps the meaning of the texts alive. The canon of scripture is technically closed, but this does not imply that the Bible is a closed system of meaning, as some contemporary canonical critics and structuralists might suggest. On the contrary, although the canon is closed, (and in this instance it does not matter which canon is being referred to), the story it conveys is incomplete and continuing, as it is presented in the worshipping community where it continues to address, judge, and transform human experience and expectation. Gabriel was convinced of the formative effect of the declaiming of scripture in the worship of the Church, and of how it enabled her to fulfil her calling to be the primary means whereby the reign of God was actualised in the world. (*Authority* p. 66).

Linking the Testaments

Having thus outlined Gabriel's basic approach to the Bible, we can return to the central question of how the two testaments might be seen to be linked together. There are many possible views to this question, but there are three specific ways of linking the two testaments in Gabriel's writings.

The first applies at the purely literary level, and concerns the complex, varied and critical ways in which the individual writers of the New Testament books actually used the Old Testament. The writers employed a whole range of literary devices to show parallels and contrasts, and this procedure had the overall effect of spinning an intricate web, and thereby creating a sense of biblical unity. This literary unity of the Bible, crafted by the New Testament writers use of allusion, metaphor, analogy and citation, is discerned by a fairly surface reading of the texts, and clearly presupposes some deeper linkage.

A second, deeper level of linkage, providing a crucial line of continuity between the two testaments, is what might be described as the shared perspective of faith. In this regard, Gabriel tells the Christian reader 'to enter into and understand the faith which inspired the ancient Israelite writers, and the authority which the tradition of their faith exercised over them'. (*Authority* p. 131)

Thus Gabriel tells how we are to share the secret of Israel's faith and hope, and that it is precisely this hope which links both testaments together, and provides the reader with the necessary presupposition for reading the Bible as scripture.

The third and strongest theological linkage between the two testaments hinges upon the conviction that God's purpose is being worked out in time and within the vicissitudes of human history. The historic experience of Israel is seen by Gabriel as being a particularly focused outworking of the divine purpose, in setting out, as it were, the contours of the divine Kingdom. This is the Kingdom which was proclaimed and actually made present in the words and actions of the historical Jesus, and which was endorsed in its universality through the Resurrection and Ascension of Christ. With the dawning of this Kingdom, the divine purpose is shown, and provides the basis from which the Christian reader can claim a unity to scripture as a whole. Borrowing the term 'homology' from the theologian Phythian Adams to describe the correlation and convergence of the two testaments, Gabriel goes on to claim that the pattern of the historic outworking of the divine purpose, under the two dispensations, is one and the same. In thus positing a parallelism of events, Gabriel is employing at this stage a kind of typology; but perhaps we ought to let him speak for himself: 'In these homologies the events of the second Redemption are treated as corresponding to the events of the first. In doing so the writers are not merely drawing an interesting parallel. They need the Old Testament story in order to see in their true context the events which had lately happened; as they go over in their minds those events, they have floating in their minds the ancient story of the deliverance from Egypt and the Covenant. The terrible events of the passion, and the experience of the first Easter, were a Crossing of the Red Sea, in which the enemy had been overwhelmed in the waters, and the Pillar of Cloud had gone before, leading the Israel of God to salvation and freedom (Authority, p. 221).

Gabriel was not averse to using the tools of critical biblical scholarship, but his approach to the Bible as scripture, most clearly exemplified in *The Throne of David* diverged significantly from the approach adopted by the majority of scholars in the theological departments of English universities. This difference of approach exhibited itself in Gabriel's contributions to the discussions of the Archbishops' Commission on Training for the Ministry, which first met in January 1937, and held its final session on 19 November 1943. At this final meeting Gabriel circulated a memorandum in which he set out his reasons why he could not endorse the proposed recommendation in the report that ordinands of the Church of England should receive their basic theological and biblical education in the theological faculties of the universities. His motive in dissociating himself from this particular recommendation was not solely an attempt to secure a future for Kelham theological college, which, in any case, had always been happy to send its more academically able students to the university after they had completed their theological course, but to underscore what he and many of his brethren saw as an important difference of approach to the Bible. In the universities, historical criticism was the stock in trade, and most biblical scholars had dismissed, or forgotten, the typological approach to scripture, which in Gabriel's mind was considered to be the most theologically productive reading of scripture.

Today we are witnessing an interesting shift and broadening of attitudes, and seeing a greater willingness on the part of biblical scholars to adopt a wider range of reading strategies alongside the traditional historical critical approach. The revival of interest in the literary composition of the canonical Bible has been stimulated in no small measure by the work of the North American scholar Northrop Frye. Interestingly, his magisterial study of biblical literature *The Great Code* (Routlege and Kegan Paul, 1982) not only restores the notion of typology, but regards it as a central interpretative key. Typology, according to Frye, is not only a hermeneutical method for eliciting the meaning from a text, but is a recurring feature of the very language of biblical literature. Increasingly biblical scholars are recognising the 'type-antitype, promise-fulfilment' structure of biblical writing, but ironically, the renewed interest in typology has been prompted by a literary theorist and not a biblical scholar. As one critic has aptly remarked, 'It is somewhat ironic that today, in the age of extremely departmentalised academic biblical scholarship, it is the task of the literary critic to call attention to the intrinsic and imaginative unity of the Bible, an idea that has been neglected by the majority of biblical scholars'.[4]

In an important essay on the nature of theology, Andrew Louth registers the fact that the work of Gabriel in the field of biblical studies has been strangely neglected.[5] Indeed, many of the points raised in contemporary discussion concerning the ways in which the Bible might serve as a resource for theological reflection were made by him over forty years ago. Gabriel repudiated, for example, the allegorical method of exegesis, on the grounds that it tended to read meanings into a text, (see Authority p.234), but he was consistent in his commitment to the traditional typological reading of scripture. For this reason his work was recognised and valued by Jean Danielou, who published a classic study of the typological exegesis in Patristic sermons and catechetical instructions; entitled *Bible et liturgie* (Cerf.) in 1951. More recently, Enrico Mazza's *Mystagogy* (Pueblo, '89) has contributed to a more general reconsideration of the typological method of biblical interpretation. In this work Mazza sets out a clear account of the typological method, a method, he says, which does not give priority to the New Testament over the Old, or the Old over the New. What is required, he suggests, is for both testaments to be continually referred to each other. 'The interpretation is a very dynamic one and consists in keeping the two Testaments interrelated in a kind of superposition of each on the other'. (*Mystagogy* p. 10). The view expressed here is reminiscent of the points which Gabriel made in his writings on the unity and interpretation of the two Testaments. By reading both Testaments together, time is telescoped and the reader is able to enter the foundational and formative story of salvation history. Methodologically, a typological reading of scripture proceeds via a comparison, matching and layering of texts to form, as it were, a template which renders visible the shape of God's saving work. At the literary level the typological method requires the discernment of poetic sequences, the so-called types and anti-types, and at the theological level, the recognition of the consistent outworking in time of God's saving drama.

Interpretation and Use of the Bible

How then are we to evaluate Gabriel's contribution to the field of biblical studies? He has been rightly associated with the so-called Biblical Theology movement which reached its zenith in British, American, and Australian university faculties of theology in the 1950s. In the autumn term of 1948 he was the Visiting English Lecturer at Berkeley Divinity School, and during that time, he

lectured extensively in Texas, Berkeley, California, Chicago, at the
General Seminary in New York, and Trinity College, in Toronto,
Canada. It was a tight and demanding schedule, and his lectures
drew out the themes expounded in his *Authority of the Old Testament* – the unity of the two testaments, and the use of the Bible in
the liturgy. The following year, Gabriel was awarded an honorary
Doctor of Divinity degree from the University of Aberdeen, largely in
recognition of his work in biblical studies. He contributed a number
of articles to Alan Richardson's *A Theological Word Book of the
Bible*, a book which has aptly been described as the English monu-
ment to biblical theology. It was first published in 1950, and ran
through eleven impressions, with the final edition being produced in
1972. Proof positive, if any were required, to show that it was an
influential theological resource book. The book itself, typical of its
kind in biblical theology circles, sought to trace out single biblical
themes and elucidate what were considered to be distinctively biblical
ideas. By the mid-1960s such an approach was increasingly seen as
being untenable, not least because the end result was invariably
abstract, resulting from a levelling of the texts and a disregard of
differences of genre and historical setting. Gabriel, it seems, was not
totaly unaware of these methodological problems. For in a later
book *Fundamentalism and the Church of God*, (SCM 1957), he
urged his readers to 'attend to the genre of each biblical writing', and
to respect the variety of literature bound together in the Bible. So,
unlike some other writers of the period, Gabriel realised the impossi-
bility of forcing the diverse literature of the Bible into a single
interpretative framework, or subsuming it under a general theme.

Gabriel's ability to discern and meet theological matters of the
moment is clearly demonstrated in his *Fundamentalism and the
Church of God*, a mature non-technical, but well considered book.
In this work he sets himself a fourfold aim: first, to critically evaluate
the phenomenon of fundamentalism as it manifests itself in the
Christian world, secondly, to discuss the cluster of issues which
surround the question of the interpretation of the Bible, and the
veracity of Christian truth-claims, thirdly, to draw together the
social and individual dimensions of Christian life and witness, and
finally, to warn against the dangers of sectarianism, and to present a
model of the catholicity of the Church, in which those who hold
radically different appoaches to scripture can be seen to coexist and
to cooperate in the Church's mission, the Church's outreach and
dialogue with the diverse social and cultural groupings in the world.

Underlying the whole book is the expressed hope of bringing conservative evangelicals and those with a more catholic outlook into a closer dialogue.

A further opportunity to bring catholic and evangelical views of scripture into dialogue, presented itself soon after the publication of *Fundamentalism*. In July 1957, Dr Davis McCaughey, the Presbyterian professor of New Testament at Ormond College, Melbourne and member of the Australian Council of the World Council of Churches, wrote to Gabriel at St Michael's House, to ask if he would take responsibility for convening an ecumenical working party in Adelaide to compile a report on the authority of the Bible for the National Conference of Australian Churches which was being planned for 1959. Davis himself was convinced that Gabriel was the most suited person to tackle the subject, and knew that he would be sensitive towards those on the proposed working party who would hold radically different viewpoints from his own. In his reply to Davis, Gabriel prevaricated. He argued that he himself was 'getting on', and that the proposed task was 'quite beyond our resources'. But in fact, although his base at St Michael's House, precariously exposed to the natural elements on the Adelaide Hills was some distance from the city, an ecumenical group, to which he belonged, had already formed itself as the Adelaide Theological Circle.

So, in many respects, Gabriel was well qualified and well placed to undertake the job, and in fact was soon persuaded to convene the group, which was formally constituted as a Faith and Order Commission working party. Gabriel was unanimously elected as chairman at the first meeting of the working party on 25 November, 1957. Arrangements were soon made to widen the process of consultation, and interested scholars in other States were able to receive and comment on the discussion papers written by members of the Adelaide based working party. These discussion papers dealt with a wide range of potentially contentious issues, such as the relation of scripture and tradition, and inerrancy and the nature of inspiration, but each was circulated widely and given adequate time for discussion. The task of actually drafting the report was left to Gabriel, who received some assistance from Donald Robinson, a noted evangelical Anglican. The report entitled 'The Authority of the Word of God: Primarily as Mediated in Holy Scripture', was published in 1959 as a study document for the National Conference of Australian Churches, which took place on – 11 February 1960, at the University of Melbourne. Recalling the memory of the process of drafting the report, Donald Robinson, who is the present Archbishop of Sydney, has said 'In my view Gabriel's courteous and persistent engagement in what he used to call "the gentle art of religious controversy" led to an important lessening of the gap between entrenched views'. The report itself directly addressed the question of the status of the Bible in the Church, and the crucial question of the relation between scripture and Christian theology, 'a problem of much urgency for us all and the whole Church'. Although the primary aim of the report was to stimulate theological discussion free from prejudice, the ecumenical implications of the subject were never far below the surface of the text, and indeed was made explicit in Gabriel's remarks in the Preface: 'The Church has had a long and tangled history. . . . It has been a glorious history, of faith and obedience . . . and it has been a history of conflict . . . there has been disobedience, false compromise and wordliness. In consequence the Church, which in its life "in Christ" is one, has become divided. It is indeed right that there should be in the Church a diversity of traditions, for unity does not at all mean uniformity; but it is wrong that the traditions should stand as rivals to one another and not be seeking to understand and to help one another'. (*Preface*, p. 2)

The Bible and Worship – A Symbiotic Relationship

Arguably, Gabriel's most significant contribution to biblical studies is to be seen in his repeated claim that the Church's liturgy provides the primary context for a Christian reading of the Bible. The Christian liturgy, he says, is the best of all schools for the study of the theological unity of the Bible. Worship, he argues, is the primary context in which the Christian can hear the meaning of scripture, and by using its vocabulary in worship, they are able to enter into that meaning and make it their own. In a passage in which he speaks of the relationship and resonance between Christian worship and the New Testament, Gabriel continues, 'So it is with the Old Testament also. We can enter into the meaning of the Old Testament as we use its words as the vehicles of our approach to God in adoration, penitence, thanksgiving and supplication, and as we ourselves tremble at the prophetic warnings of divine judgement. Hence the liturgy of the Church is the true school for the right interpretation of the Bible'. (*Authority*, p. 128)

This note is sounded again in his short study *When Israel Came Out of Egypt*, (SCM 1961). In many ways this was a remarkable little book; it made accessible to the general reader the results of critical scholarship, particularly the work of H.H.Rowley. It ends with another appeal to see the liturgy as the natural context for understanding the meaning, in this case, of the exodus story. What Gabriel seems to be saying at this point is that the ways in which scripture is is used in the worshipping traditions of the Church, for example in hymnody, and prayers provides a necessary control and guide for a Christian reading of of scripture. It is the Bible used in its primary context, setting before us the normative reading of the Bible as Christian scripture.

In this book, having first insisted that our understanding of the Bible ought to be compatible with the consensus reading of historical criticism, Gabriel reminds his readers that the first Exodus was a 'deliverance of a nation of slaves out of political servitude into freedom'. The second Exodus, fulfilled in Christ, tells how the redeemed people of God are delivered from the hold of sin and death into the liberty of the children of God. This essentially theological understanding of the Exodus, he argues, is preserved and conveyed to us in the words of the Church's liturgy. So Gabriel draws his survey to a close by saying, 'the meaning of all this is far better rendered in the sacred poetry of the Christian liturgy than in any words of ours'. (*When Israel*, p. 117)

He than illustrates his point by showing how the language of the Old Testament Exodus and that depicting the redemption wrought by the death and resurrection of Christ, are set side by side in the *Paschal Praeconium*, or the Exultet, sung at the Easter Vigil, so that the Old and New Testaments are allowed to illuminate and inform each other. This typolological juxtaposition is clearly seen in the following short extract from the *Exultet*:

> 'This is the Paschal Feast wherein the true Lamb is slain whose blood hallows the doorposts of the faithful. ... On this night which purged away the darkness of sin by the light of the fiery pillar ... On this night Christ burst the bonds of death and rose victorious from the grave ... We pray Lord, that this candle, hallowed to the honour of your name, may continue unfailingly to scatter the darkness of this night'.

Contemporary Application

Throughout his writings Gabriel provides many examples of how the liturgical use of the Bible can keep our sense of scripture alive; but there are two points in particular which would reward further attention and discussion.

First, the Bible itself is the primary, which is not to say the exclusive, resource for the vocabulary of Christian prayer and hymnody. As an example of classical hymnody, Gabriel cites 'Come, thou redeemer of the earth' (English Hymnal, 14), ascribed to Ambrose of Milan, and shows what an artful piece of writing it is with its rich tapestry of biblical allusion. This hymn, given in the English Hymnal as the Office Hymn for Christmas Eve, combines imagery from both Old and New Testaments, and echoes the psalmody associated with the Christmas season.

In particular, Gabriel draws the reader's attention to verse six:

> 'O equal to thy Father, thou!
> Gird on thy fleshly mantle now;
> The weakness of our mortal state
> With deathless might invigorate'.

Here we see a direct allusion to Psalm 93, in which 'The Lord, the King, puts on glorious apparel and girds himself with strength'. Ambrose exploits the typological correspondence, so that in terms of the hymn the 'apparel' is frail human flesh, and the 'strength' is perfected in human weakness. What is demonstrated here is an impressive weaving of biblical imagery and a thoroughgoing bibliophonic piece of liturgical writing. As such, it is certainly preferable to the tendency shown in some more recent liturgical writing of simply parroting scripture, as in the introductory sentences in the Alternative Service Book, or in serving it neat, as it were, in the form of biblicist choruses.

The provision of introductory and postcommunion sentences in the Eucharist is sometimes defended on the grounds that it makes the liturgy more scriptural; but is this really taking scripture with the seriousness it deserves? These sentences are thematically selected, invariably taken out of context, and the assumption is that they will immediately and automatically convey their meaning to the worshipping assembly. The problem has been succinctly put by Michael Kitchen in an essay on 'The Bible in Worship', in which he says that

'Bald quotation such as this may suggest an almost magical understanding of scripture'.⁶

The second point concerns the procedures we might adopt to
arrange the biblical readings and psalmody for the Church's round
of daily prayer. For two reasons *lectio continua*, the reading in
course of the whole, or greater part, of the Bible, seems better than a
more selective approach. First, the historical character of biblical
faith requires the full recital of the history of ancient Israel and of
the origins and development of primitive Christianity. Secondly, the
narrative quality of so much biblical material seems to demand a
sustained series of episodic readings. This narrative material is of
more than historic interest, for the very narrative structure serves to
locate ourselves within the plan and purposes of God. As an example
of this, Gabriel cites the stories of David, and argues that the
function of these narratives is to help the reader, and particularly
those who hear those stories declaimed, to recognise that those
stories are part of their own story. These narratives, in other words,
are a means of establishing the reader's own identity of being a
person within the people of God.

> '(The ordinary Christian) knows, or ought to know, that
> the question whether David or Elhanan slew Goliath is
> one for the specialist historian to decide. But he himself is
> well able to appreciate the meaning of the divine blessing
> which is repeatedly said to rest on David; he is described
> as "cunning in playing, and a mighty man of valour, and
> a man of war, and prudent in speech, and a comely
> person, the Lord is with him" (1 Sam.xvi, 18) ... There
> is not only the truth of the narratives as history, nor only
> the truth of the narrator's interpretation, but also the
> personal relation that exists between the characters in the
> story and those who hear it'. (*Authority*, p. 244)

When these stories are read to the gathered worshipping community,
they are heard as part of the story of the messianic people of God,
the new Israel. As Gabriel rather quaintly, but truly puts it, 'it is the
story of *our* David!'

> '... we read his story as being ourselves members of the
> Israel of God, and we accept him as being one of our
> heroes; we are asked in some measure to live through his
> experience, just as we live through the experience of the
> psalmist in reciting the psalms'. (pp. 244–5)

One frequent objection raised against the *lectio continua* arrangement is that we are exposed to too much scripture. Against this objection and the understandable worry about possible scriptural indigestion, it could be argued that the important principle underlying *lectio continua* is not that the totality of the canon needs to be rehearsed, but that each genre must be fully represented in a systematic and balanced way. Furthermore, the readings at morning and evening prayer need not be of comparative length. Indeed, the literary character of the passage could operate as the determining factor. A narrative piece of writing, for instance, requires a longer sweep, whereas passages rich in imagery could be presented in much smaller snippets. This would apply, for example, to some of the prophetic books or passages which are essentially aphoristic and epigrammatic, such as Proverbs, or the so-called Sermon on the Mount.

A similar logic might be applied to the use of the psalter in the daily offices. Gabriel recognised that some of the psalms were problematical, but maintained that the reading of the whole psalter over a given period of time was the best arrangement for providing psalmody for the daily offices. There are, of course, other possible options. One could, for example, be selective and simply provide psalms appropriate to the time of day at which the office is celebrated. What has come to be known as the people's office, as opposed to the monastic office, has historically been selective in its use of psalmody. Psalm 141, with its reference to the 'evening sacrifice' was used at Vespers, and psalm 63, which includes the phrase 'early will I seek you', was used at Mattins. So, there is considerable precedent for a selective use of psalmody, using psalms appropriate to the hour, and season of the Church's calendar, in the Church's daily prayer.

An argument against the use of the whole psalter has also been raised on the grounds that not all the material is suitable for Christian worship. Gabriel realised that for many people, the vindictive and imprecatory psalms were a stumbling block, and that psalms such as psalm 109 were incompatible with the Christian ethic of forgiveness. There are real problems here, but there are different ways of seeking a solution. The easiest, but possibly not the most satisfactory solution is to excise those psalms and passages of psalms which are considered to be irreconcilable with the Christian ethos. This was the option taken by the Anglican Church in New Zealand, with its expurgated psalter, pruned of what is considered to be unhelpful material. (cf., A New Zealand Prayer Book) On the other hand, Gabriel's suggested route through the problem follows a very different line of approach.

Liturgically speaking Gabriel was innately conservative and he was wedded to the monastic and Cranmerian legacy of saying the psalms in course. Cranmer had arranged for the whole psalter to be recited at the office on a monthly cycle. At one level the arrangement seems arbitrary and even absurd. No one would think of using a hymn book in the same way! But what seems to be at stake here is not the particular arrangement and procedure for using the psalmody at the office, but the conviction that Christians need to be exposed to the whole gamut of the psalms. In this sense, we have a parallel with what was said above concerning the principle of *lectio continua*. The psalter is a liturgical book par exellence, not only in terms of its origins, but also because of its poetic structure, which makes it amenable to recitation and musical treatment. As a whole, it embraces a multiplicity of themes, and with its range and switches of mood, it is able to give voice to the whole range of human feelings and emotions. It was one of the early Egyptian monks, Abbot Philemon, who claimed that the psalms embraced the whole of scripture, and it was originally through monastic usage that the psalms came to occupy such a privileged position in the worship of the Church.

Gabriel himself had a great fascination for the psalms. The psalter in his stall in the Great Chapel at Kelham was full of marginalia. In one of his earlier books he quotes some words of Fr Kelly on the psalms, words which clearly influenced him greatly and helped to set his own attitude to the use of psalmody in the Church's daily prayer. Fr Kelly's words seem to have a contemporary voice, and are worth quoting here: 'The psalter is an epitome of the whole religious history of humanity; its struggle to worship God; its struggle with the powers of evil, as something anti-human and dehumanizing: its recognition that evil is yet something in men; its consequent despair over its own sin and inadequacy, and over the apparent indifference of things, perhaps even of God'.[7]

To use the psalms, says Gabriel, is to face the difficulties and to enter such a struggle, but the struggle is not that of the individual Christian, but first and foremost that of Christ. Thus Gabriel assists the Christian reader, hesitant and unsure about the use of the psalter, by reminding them that in its daily prayer the Church voices the prayer of Christ. He recalled that the opening versicle of mattins, the monastic night office, is *Domine labia mea aperies*, that is, 'O Lord, thou shalt open my lips', and goes on to explain in *The Throne of David*, 'that is, not the lips of the individual worshipper, but the lips of the Christ who now begins to praise God by the mouth of the members of his Church'. (p. 253)

So, following Gabriel's line of argument, it is Christ alone who can utter, 'Lord, how I love thy law: It is my meditation all the day long' (Psalm 119:97), and to recognise this fact soon dispels any sense of complacent self-righteousness, either feared or imagined. Similarly, if for instance, the reader recoils at the vindictive sentiments expressed in Psalm 109 – 'He clothed himself with cursing as his coat, may it soak into his body like water, like oil into his bones!' – the reader needs to recall the fact that the meaning of these sentiments shifts on the lips of Christ. As Gabriel says, He has looked into the depths of the mystery of iniquity, and the reader needs to realise that there are periods in human history, such as the period in which he was writing during the Second World War, 'when satanic evil unmasks itself' (*The Throne of David*, p. 255). What we can draw from Gabriel's line of argument here, is that Christians need to open themselves, however shocking or disconcerting some might find it, to the full gamut of human experience, and to the full and potent images of divine grace and judgement provided in the psalmody.

Accepting such a 'givenness' might well result in liberating Christians from their own subjectivity, and correct their tendency to construct a picture of God commensurate with their own sensitivities and predilections. By such an openness to the whole range of scripture, through readings and psalmody, the notion of God is preserved in all its biblical realism, and the Christian's understanding of the propensity of the human heart for both good and evil is widened beyond our imaginings. But is this too much to bear? It was T.S.Eliot who once said that human beings could not bear too much reality, but it was one of his friends and spiritual mentors, Gabriel Hebert, who assures us that we can bear such reality when we take our place within the worshipping community and offer prayer and praise to the Father, through the Son, and in the power of the Holy Spirit.

Epilogue
by PETER HINCHLIFF

GABRIEL HEBERT was, perhaps, at his most influential in the late 1950s and the 1960s. He had been born in 1886 so that he was no longer, by any stretch of the imagination, a young man when that period commenced. Nor is the claim that that was the time when he was most influential intended to deny that he contributed a great deal to earlier decades. But all the things that he stood for – ecumenism, liturgical renewal, biblical theology – seemed somehow typical of those supremely vivid and optimistic years. It was a time when those proverbial opposites, the spirit and the structure, the form and the content, seemed to belong together as never before. Those who longed for the spirit of personal love to become concrete in detailed plans for reunion; those who ached for worship to be embodied in a corporate but vital liturgy; those who hoped to hear God speak to them personally through the critically understood text of scripture; all these, during that decade, thought their dreams to be about to be realised. And for many of them it was Gabriel Hebert who had first sowed the seeds of hope.

Most of us experienced the sixties: Hebert helped to create them. Books like *Liturgy and Society*, *The Throne of David*, and *The Authority of the Old Testament* were written long before. But many of us had been brought up on them. They had helped to form our ideas and, later, when liturgical renewal or biblical theology came along they seemed nostalgically familiar in spite of their newness.

Of course the reality was not quite like the expectation. Not long ago I heard an undergraduate say, 'Oh, he is socially concerned and all those other sixties things.' He may, for all I know, have been speaking of myself. And, though I still remember the 1960s as a period of excitement, renewal and hope, I understand why others (and particularly those who did not live through them) may now think of them as naive, over-excited, trendy, the theological equivalent of Carnaby Street. There has been so much disillusionment. The steam seems to have gone out of the ecumenical movement. 'Schemes' for reunion have failed. Relations have improved between the Churches and perhaps we have got all we need. The liturgical movement has done its work and it has become fashionable to say that we need a more varied diet than the purely family-eucharistic parish communion pattern. Clergymen whose principal Sunday service is a sung eucharist at 10am can be heard saying that when they are on holiday what they like is a quiet 1662 at 8am with only half-a-dozen silently bowed heads in the congregation. Most difficult of all, we have come to think of biblical theology as having been too disconnected from critical scholarship. It was all very well for us to say that our job was to expound the teaching of a particular passage (which we had probably read as one of the lections for the day). But unless we were able to root the passage, to say how it related to Jesus of Nazareth or to the communities of the first Christians, why should that teaching possess an authority? But, here as in the other themes which Hebert explored and commended, the problem is not simply that we have become tired of them. It is also that a good deal of what he and his disciples campaigned for has passed into the common life and practice of the Church. It is now almost unusual to hear a sermon which is not, at least in theory, an exposition of one or more of the lections.

There is, of course, no period of history which seems so over-rated as the one from which we have just escaped. At any moment we may expect to see a debunking volume, called *Eminent Early Elizabethans*, emerge from some publishing house. It is, therefore, extremely difficult to write a memoir of a figure like Hebert and do him justice. To treat him as an important and influential person is to run the risk of being accused of ignoring the warts. To debunk him would be unjust. It is therefore a very considerable achievement that the present volume has managed to present Hebert as a real human being, warts and all, who nevertheless grappled with a great many important ideas, was involved in many historically significant movements and episodes, and made his contemporaries and the subsequent generations do some serious thinking.

My own reaction to reading the volume in typescript was chiefly to realise, as never quite before, how much Hebert was a product of the Society of the Sacred Mission. Father Kelly had his own warts, of course. He could be insecure, tiresome and, no doubt, infuriating. But some of the things he believed in most passionately had a kind of visionary quality and one can, I think, detect their influence on

Hebert's thought. Kelly's idea of 'the catholicity of God' was something like omnipresence touched with universalism and given a quality of richness by a sense of tradition. At the same time Kelly's idea of catholicity was never one which treated tradition as if it were a repository for rigid and unchanging rules. His catholicism was always a rational, sensible catholicism. And, finally, Kelly was never much interested in academic theology for its own sake: his concern was always for a theology which sprang out of and, in turn, illuminated the prayer and the practical life of Christian people.

Much of Hebert's thinking and writing seems to depend upon a very similar vision of the nature of God and so also of the nature of theology and a 'catholic' discipline of life. Trying to live by these perceptions was not always smooth and simple. Sometimes a sense of the catholicity of God and of the rationality of catholic theology might cause Hebert to lean in one direction in the debate about intercommunion. At another time, the realities of life within a particular Christian body with its own discipline, liturgy and corporate character embodied in a tradition, might cause him to lean in the other direction. That was not so much a contradiction in his character as a symptom of the way in which the practical demands of life made it impossible to be wholly consistent about real as opposed to academic theology. His theological concerns were always very practical. Liturgy for him was not an archaic study or a branch of aesthetics. Ecumenism was worked out with real people, whether Swedes or Australians. That said, however, one suspects that his idiosyncrasies did sometimes leave their mark upon his theology. He, too, was one of the realities of life.

If it is true that much of what Hebert stood for has passed into the common life of the Church, and not just the Anglican Church; and if it is true that some of the things for which he campaigned are now thought of as not worth bothering about, is any of it still of real interest thirty years on? There are all sorts of reasons why it should be so. In the first place, merely as a matter of keeping the record straight, it is important that his place in recent history should be recognized. Secondly, his own catholicism, rational, sensible, and clear-eyed, valued self-criticism. If some of the enthusiasms of the sixties turned out to be mere trendiness, Hebert himself would have wished us to say so – probably in an impish, mischievous tone of voice. Thirdly; the wheel turns and sometimes turns far more quickly than one would have supposed possible. Contemporary enthusiasm for what is called post-modernism is already making it possible to rehabilitate some aspects of biblical theology or at least to present it in a more respectable light. Even if every writer who calls him- or herself a post-modernist defines post-modernism differently, the one thing they all have in common is a rejection of the characteristic Englightenment conviction that all knowledge had, and must have, a rational, empirical basis. In a world where that was still the common assumption, some biblical theology may sometimes have seemed, as I have argued, to have lacked a rationale. Now we understand hermeneutics rather differently and defining the precise authority upon which an interpretation rests no longer seems of such vital importance. A post-modern biblical theology sometimes seems not at all far off. And some of the other concerns, which seem to us so characteristically sixties and, for my undergraduate friend, not worth bothering about, may be back in fashion more quickly than we sometimes suppose.

But, in a sense, none of these reasons – the argument from history, the need for self-criticism, the passing of fashion – is the real one. Nor are these the reasons Hebert himself would have advanced. The truth is that in three areas vital for our everyday Christian life we still need the bringing together of the spirit and the structure. Without a properly designed structure the enthusiasm of the spirit runs to waste like blood spilled from a body which is left lifeless. The adoring love which we long to offer God in our worship needs a carefully designed form which is expressive of our common social life. If we desire to hear the word of God speaking to us we need to hear it in the text of Scripture but not in some slavish literalist sense for it needs to talk to us about our life today. If we are ever to be one, as Christ and his Father are one – which is to say 'in love' – then we shall need to discover the appropriate constitutional design to provide a vehicle for that love. Each generation, no doubt, requires a somewhat different structure. That is a necessary implication of saying that the structure has to be appropriate to the realities of the society in which we live. The task that Hebert was anxious that his generation should tackle is therefore one that can never be thought of as completed and in need of no revision. What he told us that we needed then, we still need now.

PETER HINCHLIFF
Christ Church, Oxford

Notes

Chapter 1 A Catholic Character

1. A. G. Hebert, *Liturgy and Society* Faber and Faber 1935, pp. 13–14.
2. H. A. Kennedy, in *The Horbury Parish Magazine* vol.xxxii, No.9, Sept. 1913
3. AGH in *The Anglican* 26 June 1959
4. AGH in *The Horbury Magazine* September 1913
5. cited by P.Hinchliff, *The Anglican Church in South Africa* DLT 1963, p. 210
6. AGH Personal – *Letters Sent* SSM Archives
7. AGH, *Intercommunion* SPCK 1932, p. 79
8. Dr Davis McCaughey – *Private Papers* Melbourne

Chapter 2: The Scandinavian Connection

1. A. G. Hebert, *Apostle and Bishop* Faber and Faber 1963, p. 88
2. G. C. A. Bell, *Documents of Christian Unity, 1920–24* OUP 1924, p.3
3. AGH, *The Present Grouping of Christendom: The Scandinavian Communions* SPCK & CLA 1940, p. 12
4. R. Taft, 'Receiving Communion – a Forgotten Symbol?' in *Beyond East and West: Problems in Liturgical Understanding* Pastoral Press 1984, p. 108
5. H. M. Waddams, 'Recent Developments in Swedish Theology and Church Life', in *Church Quarterly Review*, July-September 1937, p. 283
6. AGH, *Intercommunion* SPCK 1932, p. 95
7. G. Aulén, *Christus Victor* SPCK 1931, translator's preface, p. x

Chapter 3: Ecumenism and Worship

1. *The Anglican* 26 June 1956
2. quoted by S. Neill and Ruth Rouse in *A History of the Ecumenical Movement 1519–1949*, SPCK 1954, p. 437
3. A. G. Hebert, to Reginald Tribe, Letters Sent, SSM Archives
4. Herbert Kelly, *No Pious Person* Faith Press 1960, p. 115
5. G. K. A. Bell, *Documents of Christian Unity*: Second Series, Oxford 1930, p. 153
6. A. G. Hebert, *Intercommunion: A theological study of Christian Unity* SPCK 1932, p. 86
7. AGH, 'Open Communion', *The Church Quarterly Review* No. CCXLIII, April-June 1936, p. 44
8. Ibid. p. 42
9. Ibid. p. 40
10. 'Friends of Reunion', SSM Archives, AGH Private Papers
11. *Church Times*, 19 July 1963
12. AGH, 'Some Thoughts about Christian Unity', *SSM Quarterly* March 1950
13. *The Manchester Guardian* 19 July 1935
14. William Temple, letter to AGH, May 30, 1944; Lambeth Library: Temple Collection, vol. 219
15. Op. cit. p. 135
16. A. G. Hebert, *Apostle and Bishop* Faber and Faber 1963, p. 150

17. Op. cit. p. 76
18. Gustav Aulén, *Eucharist and Sacrifice* trans. E.H.Wahistom, Muhlenberg 1958 p. 37
19. A. G. Hebert, *God's Kingdom and Ours*, SCM Press 1959, p. 180

Chapter 4: Liturgical Renewal

1. W. Frere *Principles of Liturgical Reform* Murray 1911, p. 187
2. 'Letter to Bishop of Ripon, 18.11.1918,' in *Walter Howard Frere: His Correspondence on Liturgical Revision* ed. R.C.J.Jasper, SPCK/Alcuin 1954, p. 64
3. see *Theology* vol.XXXVII, No. 218, August 1938
4. see *Christendom* vol.III, No. 12, December 1933
5. A. G. Hebert *Liturgy and Society*, Faber and Faber 1935, p. 7
6. quoted in *Beauduin: A Prophet Vindicated* Sonja Quitslund, Newman Press p. 25
7. F. Gavin 'Contemporary Religion in Germany', *Theology* vol.XIX, No. 113, November 1929
8. W. Jardine Grisbrooke 'Oblation at the Eucharist: the Liturgical Issues', *Studia Liturgica* vol. 4, 1965
9. The editorial, *Modern Churchman*, vol.XXV, No. 9, December 1935
10. T. Beeson, *The Church of England in Crisis* Mowbray 1973 p.73
11. A. M. Ramsey 'The Parish Communion' *Durham Essays and Reviews* SPCK 1956

Chapter 5: The Bible and Worship

1. 'The Roman Catholic Eucharistic Lectionary', Claude Wiener, *Studia Liturgica* vol. 21, No. 1, 1991
2. E. H. Van Olst, *The Bible and Liturgy* Eerdmans 1991
3. A. G. Hebert, 'The Bible in the Church', *SSM Quarterly* Lent 1946
4. Tibor Fabiny, *The Lion and the Lamb: Figurism and Fulfilment in the Bible, Art and Literature* MacMillan 1992 p. 10
5. Andrew Louth, *Discerning the Mystery*, Clarendon Press 1983 p. 109n
6. *The Identity of Anglican Worship* edited by K. Stevenson and B. Spinks, Mowbray 1991 p. 39
7. A. G. Hebert, *Intercommunion*, SPCK 1932 p. 101

A Select Bibliography of the Writings of Gabriel Hebert

Ecclesiology and Ecumenism:
    Intercommunion, (SPCK, 1932)
    Unity in the Truth, (SPCK, 1939)
    The Form of the Church, (Faber, 1944)
    The Form of the Church, revised edition, (Faber, 1954)
    God's Kingdom and Ours, (SCM, 1959)
    Apostle and Bishop, (Faber, 1963)

articles, etc.
    'Open Communion', *Church Quarterly Review*, No. CCXLIII,
        April–June 1936
    'Rome and Reunion', *Theology*, vol. XXXVI No. 211, 1938
    'Ministerial Episcopacy', in *The Apostolic Ministry*, edited by
        K. Kirk, (Hodder and Stoughton, 1946)
    'Reflections on The Apostolic Ministry', *Theology*, vol. LIV
        No. 378, 1951
    editor: *Bulletin Oecumenique Anglican*, 1952
    'The Uniting Church', *Scottish Journal of Theology*, vol. 17 No.
        1, 1964

Worship and Liturgy:
    Liturgy and Society, (Faber, 1935)
    editor: *The Parish Communion*, (SPCK, 1937)
    with N. Allenby, *Pray with the Church*, (SPCK, 1938)
    An Essay in Baptismal Revision, (Dacre, 1947)

articles, etc.
    'Concelebration', *Theology*, vol. XXII No. 128, 1931
    'The Meaning of the Epiclesis', *Theology*, vol. XXVII No. 160,
        1933
    'Anaphora and Epiclesis', *Theology*, vol. XXXVII, No. 218, 1938
    'Anglican Worship', *Ways of Worship: The Report of a Theological Commission of Faith and Order*, (SCM, 1951)

'The Mystery of the People of God', *The Parish Communion Today*, ed. David Paton, (SPCK, 1962)

'Worship in the Old Testament', *True Worship*, ed. L. Sheppard, (DLT, 1963)

'Liturgical Prayer', *Studia Liturgica*, vol. 2 1963

Biblical Studies:

The Throne of David, (Faber, 1941)

Scripture and Faith, (Centenary Press, 1947)

The Authority of the Old Testament, (Faber, 1947)

The Bible From Within, (OUP, 1950)

Fundamentalism and the Church of God, (SCM, 1957)

When Israel Came Out of Egypt, (SCM, 1961)

articles, etc.

'Atone', 'Memory', etc. in the *Theological Word Book of the Bible*, ed. A. Richardson, (SCM, 1950)

Introduction to *The Root of the Vine: Essays in Biblical Theology*, ed. Anton Fridrichsen, (Dacre, 1953)

Translations of Swedish Theology:

Y. Brilioth, *Eucharistic Faith and Practice: Evangelical and Catholic*, in 1930

G. Aulen, *Christus Victor*, in 1931

A. Nygren, *Agape and Eros*, (vol. 1), 1932

N. Soderblom, *The Mystery of the Cross*, in 1933

INDEX